THE FABULOUS WIFE

Trish M

Cover Design: Dream Design Graphics

Interior Design: Trish M Enterprises

Cover Photo Composite: Alanna Rose Photography

Editor: Dena Marie Ramos

ISBN:
978-0-9897064-3-8

DEDICATION

      This book is dedicated to the man whom I have spent more than half of my life with…my high school sweetheart, my rock, the one who helps me to be a better me each and every day of my life. Doing life with you has taught me to be a better wife. There is so much about you that I love, honor, and adore. You compliment me so well. I thank God for creating you just for me. You are my strength. Thank you for being a wonderful husband, father, and friend. You're not just wonderful…you are the epitome of a FABULOUS husband! The love that I have for you is indescribable. May God bless us with our forever. I love you so much!

ACKNOWLEDGMENTS

First and foremost, I must give honor and glory to God. Without Him, I wouldn't even be here to share the joy of the Lord which gave me the strength to overcome and live long enough to tell somebody else how they can do it as well.

Again, to the love of my life...my always and forever...my rock, my husband...Mr. Derrick Morrissette, I love you so much.

And last, but certainly not least, to all of my family and friends who have been there by my side...I love and appreciate you so much.

CONTENTS

Introduction

Living the Dream

Living the Dream

Let's face it. Every girl's dream is to have a king come and sweep her off her feet so that she can become his queen. A queen in a huge, luxurious, and super fabulous castle with a king in charge is the American dream that almost every girl desires, or it just me? There's nothing wrong with that, right?

I remember growing up and thinking how beautiful it is to be a woman who has a man—not just any man, but a husband who loves and supports her, who cherishes her. Everyone wants to have the dream life of living happily ever after! But what exactly does that look like?

As I sit and think about that question, I ponder on the examples that I had as a child. I grew up with both parents in the home, and I have somewhat of a big family. I'm the only girl with five brothers! Yeah…I know…I know! But listen…right now, let's focus on the married examples that I had when I was a child.

Let's see. Where exactly do I start? Well, I'll just start directly in my home with my very own parents. My mom and dad were together for over 20 years! Did you catch the word "were"? Yeah, it happened. The big "D" word. Divorce came in and utterly destroyed what they had, unfortunately. That can break the heart of any kid, no matter how old they are.

When my parents divorced, I was in college. Things were always a bit crazy at home, so seeing them divorce wasn't necessarily a shocker, but it still hurt. You know why? Because in the fairy tales, nobody ever got divorced! Are you kidding me? They always lived happily ever after! So why was it that my family experienced the divorce?

My mom was an awesome woman of God who had met her prince charming (my dad) in high school. He swept her off her feet, and before they knew it, they were pregnant with their first child together (that'd be me). Shortly after that, they were married. They were young and in love, ready to spend their "forever" together, or so it seemed.

My dad was the only man that my mom had been with in her life at that time. My dad, on the other hand, let's just say he was a Slick Rick—very smooth, suave, debonair, and had a way with words and a way with the ladies! He was tall, not dark, but handsome. That's my daddy! Forever young and forever the man! And nobody could tell him differently.

Throughout their marriage, there were many ups and downs: arguments, fights, and infidelity. I had a distorted look of what marriage looked like. Could this be what happily ever after was? Was this what I had to look forward to?

Through all that happened with my dad, I can honestly say that I love him with all of my heart. My dad was a wonderful provider for his family. I loved his hard work and diligence. To this day, he's still a hard worker. He now loves taking care of his grandkids more so than the kids as we are all grown and independent now, but taking care of his family was one of my dad's greatest assets.

Getting back to the marriage, though, I guess I can say that looking at my parent's marriage didn't really inspire me to get married; however, I still had a desire to do it. My parents really loved one another, but sometimes how that love was expressed made me question it as a child. I didn't know any better. All I knew was what I saw. Is that how love was expressed? There had to be more to marriage than what I saw and experienced as a child. I just knew it! I was willing to find "the more" that I was seeking.

It wasn't just within my own house. I began to look all around me at what marriage looked like with other family members as well. I looked at uncles who were always getting drunk and getting caught with other women, while their wives stuck with them through it all. I heard or saw abuse—verbal, emotional, and at times physical— with people throughout my family. Where was the marriage that actually stood out from the rest? Could it exist? Or was this simply all a fairy tale…something that you saw on TV?

Speaking of TV…what were the examples that I saw there? Hmm…let me think. I grew up watching soap operas like *The Young and the Restless, Guiding Light, As the World Turns,* and *One Life to Live.* Yeah, I was a soap opera geek. That was because I hung around my grandmothers so much, and that's all they watched! They loved it! So, I got caught up in the foolishness. It really was foolishness, and I got caught up in the hype of it all as a young kid. The relationships on those soap operas were so dramatic! One minute, marriages were perfect. The next minute, there was lying, cheating, and sometimes murder! Are you serious right now?! Is that what I had to look forward to?

Seeing a good example of what marriage was supposed to look like was very hard to find, yet so many of us wanted it. It's like it was embedded in us within our DNA. That was the life, right? After all, the word of God says that it's not good for man to be alone (Genesis 2:18). God said that He would make man a helper suitable for him called "woman". The woman was called and destined to be the wife of a man. It's who God called us to be, ladies; that's why we can't help desiring it!

So God said He would send man someone "suitable". What is a wife that is suitable? Well, according to dictionary.com, suitable is "appropriate, fitting, or becoming." Now, I must say, the word "becoming" stuck out to me in the definitions. If I am suitable to be a wife, then I *become* the wife. Why does suitable mean becoming? Becoming (according to dictionary.com) is all about "a process of change, any change involving realization of potentialities, as a movement from the lower level of potentiality to the higher level of actuality". So wait…after you become the wife that's suitable, you now have to go through this phase of "becoming" the wife? Yes, you have to go through this phase of DAILY changing into a better you, helping the husband to become a better him, while you go from a lower level to a higher level of growth and actuality, which simply means that you evolve daily in becoming the best wife that you can be! Now that's deep, dictionary.com! That helped me out! You see, you are suitable to be married, but you have to *become* what he needs every day of his life so that you both can become who you need to be in this thing called life! Yesssss!

𓅓𓅓

In order to be a fabulous wife, you have to evolve daily, grow daily, become daily....

✝

So here's a great point to put in the introduction of this book. In order to be a fabulous wife, you have to evolve daily, grow daily, become daily. You have to work daily on becoming the best YOU that you can be so that you can help him be the best that he can be. You are called to the position of help. God called you to be a "helpmate". A helpmate is simply "anyone who aids or assists regularly" (dictionary.com). Listen, some days you may not feel like it, and I get it; however, I want you to think about it like this. Some days, you may not feel like going to work, but in order to keep your job, you show up daily! You want to keep a good marriage, right? Then you better make sure you show up daily for work…because it sure is work! That's one of the things that you have to do as a fabulous wife. You have to show up daily with all your fabulosity! Yes! That's your job. That's what makes you suitable. That's what makes you irresistible! You know how to show up for your husband, even when you don't feel it!

Being married is not a feeling. Being a wife is not a feeling, either. It's a position in life that you have to take seriously every single day. You have to show up for your position, but don't just show up. Actually be present in your marriage! Going through the motions of being married…going through the motions of being a wife…that's not going to work. You have to be in it to win it! Living the fairytale life requires work. It requires you showing up daily to your job and doing what you have been called and chosen to do. Being a fabulous wife is a decision that you have to make daily.

The dream of being a wife is free. The hustle and everyday work of being a wife is sold separately. The hustle is going to COST you something. Are you sure you're ready to pay the cost?

Being a fabulous wife takes work. Oftentimes, it's the kind of work that many women just honestly aren't ready for. The dream of marriage is beautiful. The hustle of marriage can be ugly if you let it. So why do we want it so badly?

Marriage has existed longer than written history. If I were to ask 50 college girls where they saw themselves in ten years, they would more than likely answer married, with kids, with a certain type of job/income, etc. Marriage is an integral part of our culture. With marriages failing at nearly 50 percent, and with the multitude of unhappy marriages in existence, why do people still want to get married so badly? Cultural tradition and expectations, the desire to possess another and the idea of being a king or queen for a day are at the root of most people's desire to marry. I have a question for you. Why did you get married? Or, if you're single, why do you want to get married. Is it just something on your bucket list, or it something that you have a strategic plan for?

One of the things that I have found over the years is that many people don't take marriage as seriously as they should. They think that just because they love someone, then they should marry them, right? You're so wrong! You see, marriage has to be based on more than just love. Think about it this way: If all it took was love for a marriage to last, then I'm positive that there wouldn't be as many divorces all over the world. You know why? For those that got a divorce, the vast majority of them still LOVED their spouse to a certain degree. It may not be that hot and on-fire love that they started out with as newlyweds, but there's still love there for their significant other.

Love will never be enough. To have a fabulous marriage and to be a fabulous wife, it goes way deeper than just the concept of LOVE.

Don't get me wrong, love is extremely important. But to have a long, strong, healthy marriage, more than love is required. And I'm excited to share with you in this book what it takes to be considered a fabulous wife who has a fabulous marriage. Now listen, being fabulous and having a fabulous marriage doesn't mean perfection. No, no, no. That's not what I'm saying at all. Through all of the imperfections, you learn how to have a lifestyle of fabulosity.

I want to help you accomplish that!

Who am I, you might ask? Well, I guess now will be a perfect time to introduce myself—after all, this is the introduction of the book!

My name is Trish Morrissette. I was born and raised in a small city called Jackson, Alabama, (Toddtown area to be exact). I am the only girl out of six children. My parents had 4 children together, and my dad (with his extracurricular activities) had 2 more boys outside of my mom. As stated earlier, my parents ended up divorcing after 20 plus years together. The entire time I was growing up, I had both parents in the house.

In high school, I dated a few guys—not many; however, I did end up dating "the guy". You know, the one that takes your breath away, knocks you off your feet, and allows you to see and experience another level that none of the other guys could compare to…yeah, that one!

In essence, I'm referring to my high school sweetheart, my one and only, my best friend, my ace boon coon, my purpose partner, my life partner, my soulmate…the one that no other man could ever compare to. He's not perfect, but he's all mine! Let me introduce you to my king. His name is Derrick. He put the "M" on Trish M. He makes my heart sing. He rocks my boat and gives me butterflies. After all these years of being together, he still knows how to make this girl blush!

Derrick and I have been together for decades, and we still have our lifetime to go. We've gone through our share of ups and downs, but we have been able to overcome many obstacles by the grace of God!

We both chose to show up for work daily…you know…in this thing called "marriage". We can't see doing this thing called life with anyone else. That's one of the signs to let you know that this thing is REAL. But hold on, ladies. That feeling has to be mutual! You can't be walking around talking about doing life with someone who only wants to do dates with you! Ouch!!! Come on now! That will preach! But wait, let me get back to where I was.

Derrick and I have been married for decades. We have two miracle babies, a son and a daughter (DaeShaun and Daesha). I say "miracles" because we endured so much to have them. You would have to go back and read my first book, *Faith in a Barren Land*, to understand what I'm saying. It was a miracle! I was pregnant eight times. I had six miscarriages (and I almost died from the first one). My son was pregnancy number five. He is our first-born. My daughter was pregnancy number eight. Everything before and in between them all resulted in miscarriages, which was one of the hardest things that we endured during our marriage.

Don't get me wrong; I'm going to have plenty of things to share with you on our struggles. These are the same struggles that helped me to understand how to walk in all my fabulosity while being married to this awesome man. Every day, I learn more about how to be more fabulous than I was the day before. My goal is to remind him daily of who I am. When he sees me, he sees fabulous! When he experiences me, he experiences all of my fabulosity! That's not to say I won't have a bad day, but for the most part, my goal is to work on being the best me that I can possibly be for this mighty man that God has sent me!

You see, I'm just a woman trying to live the dream. The dream of happiness. The dream of destiny. The dream of being happy.

I know that you are desiring the same thing as well.

It's not good for any man or woman to be alone. God told us that in His Word. You want to be happy and live the dream too! Yes, I already know! However, I want to challenge you on something right here, right now. I challenge you to know and understand what your definition of "happy wife" is. What does you being a happy wife look like, sound like and even seem like? Whatever it is, are you prepared to teach your husband how to make you happy?

Some may find that question weird. I know. But did you know that it really is important to teach your husband how to love you? What exactly is your love language? What does it take to make you happy? Have you ever experienced happiness to the fullest extent in your marriage? What does that look like? Or what does that NOT look like?

Listen, throughout this book, I want you to evaluate YOU. I want you to think about how you can take YOU being a wife to the next level. I know many of you will say something about him and what he needs to do and how he needs to do it. Stop right there. This book is NOT about him! This book is about YOU!

We're not going to finger-point in this book. Let's face it. You could probably write a long list of how he needs to change and some things that he can do better. NEWS FLASH...this book is not about the fabulous husband. It's about the fabulous wife!

When you decide to change and go to the next level, then everything around you changes. You just have to simply choose to do so. Everything changes when you change. So, that's my goal. You may already be a great wife, but hear me good: THERE'S ALWAYS A NEXT LEVEL

You can never become great if you're always settling for good. Being a good wife is no longer acceptable. We're working on being FABULOUS!

When you realize that you can be more, then be it.

No more score cards to see if you're outdoing him in an area. It doesn't matter if you are or not. Are you counting scores like it's a game or something? NEWS FLASH...being married is not a game. Your spouse is not your opponent. You're actually on the same team. You have to purpose in your heart to win together, not make one feel like a loser when they get around you.

The goal is to win TOGETHER.

The goal is to go to the next level TOGETHER.

My prayer is that after reading this book, you are ready to do just that. We've got work to do, ladies. Now let's work on walking in a greater level of fabulosity...TOGETHER!

Get ready to be held accountable. This book is going to challenge who you are as a wife, but don't worry...it's for your GOOD!

Chapter 1

The Journey Begins

The Journey Begins

I remember it like it was yesterday. We were in high school. It was our junior year, around Christmas time. My husband (then boyfriend), decided to get me something special that year. We were sitting in my living room on the couch. My parents were in their room watching TV, and my brothers were in their room as well. Derrick and I were sitting down enjoying those quiet moments together. We were just two teenagers who were absolutely crazy about each other! I know you're thinking we were too young for that, but I beg to differ! We truly loved one another. I knew my husband was the one when we were dating in high school. He was just different. We had such a special connection; it was one that I had never had with anyone else. I know...I know...I didn't really get a whole lot of experience under my belt, but it was enough! Enough to know that I had the real one on my hands!

So, we were sitting on the couch in the living room, and he handed me this cute little wrapped box. Immediately, my mind began to wonder what in the world it was! It looked like a ring box, but it could have easily been earrings, right? Then I began to think that if it was a ring, we were a little too young to be talking about marriage! But anyway....my heart rejoiced! I began smiling ear to ear allowing him to see the joy that I had upon receiving that cute little box! "What's this?" I asked in astonishment. Smiling from ear to ear, I began to tear off the layers on the outside of it, and guess what it was? It was a cute little ring! It was soooooooo adorable! Let me explain to you how it looked. It was a 24-carat gold ring that had a heart in the middle of it. In the middle of the heart was this little bitty diamond (I'm pretty sure it was a cubic zirconia, though). I saw the diamond. I saw the heart in the middle. I thought to myself how he had to be really digging me like I was digging him in order for him to buy me this cute little ring! I was blushing, thinking how lucky I was to have a guy buy me a ring for Christmas!

Now, I knew it wasn't expensive, but it was real, and it was mine! It was more like a promise ring to me, but I took it as an engagement ring more than anything. I couldn't help myself. I had to ask. I looked at him with beaming eyes and said, "So, does this mean that you want to marry me one day?" Okay, pause right there. Let me just give you some quick details about me. For one, I never dated just to be "dating". I always dated with the purpose or intent to marry the one that I was dating. Of course, he had to be the right one in order for that to happen. I truly felt like Derrick was the one (and of course, I was right!).

So, after asking Derrick if he wanted to marry me one day, he immediately let me know that I was correct in my assumptions. He looked at me with a shy grin on his face and said, "Yes, you're my girl." Okay, so here I go blushing to the next level! Oh, this guy had game because I was so gone!! I know this is hilarious, but I got to tell my story!

After Derrick stated that he definitely wanted to marry me, I had this really genius idea run through my head! I knew what he could do! I instantly told him my idea! "So, if you really want to marry me, why don't you propose the old-fashioned way. Just come out and ask me if that's what you really want to do." I know telling him this was pretty bold, right? But if you know me and you know my personality, you'd know that I'm a pretty bold lady! I don't hold a lot of things back. So, I told him what was on my mind. I let him know that if that's what he was thinking, that we should marry one day, then I needed him to officially propose to me. Do it old school! Get down on one knee! Take it to another level!! Okay, I'm real EXTRA, but I love it!

So, he looked at me and smiled. "I have no problem doing that", he said. He got down on one knee, and he proposed to me! "Demetrish Dickinson (my full maiden/legal name), will you marry me?" At this point, I really wanted to cry! He was truly a sweetheart.

I accepted his proposal and gave him a kiss. "Yes, I will absolutely marry you, Sir!" I hugged his neck to let him know how truly grateful I was for this moment. We then began to talk about our plans for marriage. Of course, we weren't able to do that at such a young age, but we did talk about how we wanted to finish high school and college and then make it happen. Until then, I would wear that promise ring everywhere I went to represent our young, but yet strong love for one another!

Derrick and I were young. We were in love. We were high school sweethearts. We were popular in school. I was a star athlete, and so was he. We really had great things going for us.

Growing up, I can say that I was really spoiled. I was the only girl in the family, and my dad made sure he spoiled his only girl! My mom was giving, too, but I could get more out of my dad with just one look! I call that the "only girl power"! My brothers hated it! But hey, what can I say? It was five of them and only one of me. I considered myself very special! It was nothing for me to have the latest sneakers, jerseys, jeans, etc. I was a fashionista, even at a young age. In my younger years, I was more of a tomboy, but I still liked to dress up. I liked looking cute and jazzy. Not only that, I was riding in a brand-new vehicle at the age of 15! I didn't even have a license yet, but I had a car! And a new one at that! My parents took really good care of me. We weren't rich, but they made a way with what they had. If we ever struggled with anything, I never knew it. My dad was a great provider, and he worked really hard at taking care of the home and making sure we were all good. My mom worked hard as well. She worked and went to school in order to get her degree in nursing. She was diligent and determined to finish, and she did just that!

My husband, on the other hand, grew up slightly different. I remember him telling us stories of how they didn't have lights or running water often times in their home. Things were challenging financially for his family growing up, but they always worked with what they had. They lived in run-down homes until they were finally able to afford a better one. He talked about the struggles that they had often, and how he was so grateful to finish school and go on to college and get a degree.

My husband is a wonderful provider. He takes great care of our home, making sure we all are good. He often tells our kids about how he grew up, and how he didn't have the luxuries that they have. We teach our kids to be grateful to God for everything. Many people don't have what they have. The lessons that my husband and I learned as kids have spilled over into our adult life tremendously. We are so grateful to God for what He has done!

Even though my parents often gave me money, I still wanted my own. In high school, I got a j-o-b as soon as I turned 16 when I could work and get my license. I remember working at Hardee's during my high school years. I would hurry from practice to work, then to home or to go hang out with my "boo" depending on what day of the week it was. I was always willing to work hard for what I wanted in life. I never stopped working since the age of 16. I used the money I made to buy myself and Derrick gifts, or I would use it to hang out and eat; however, I never really saved anything. I was pretty bad at that. I didn't learn about saving until later on after marriage, and my husband would fuss about me always spending and not saving ANYTHING! That's all I knew how to do.! We'll talk about that later in the MONEY chapter.

Having financial goals and being on one accord is critical in a marriage. If one has bad habits and the other doesn't, it's important for the one with the bad habits to admit when they are wrong—that's in ANY area. See what you're doing wrong and work hard at being better so your goals can be met.

It was exciting graduating from high school together. We had such great memories. From going to proms, to playing ball, to senior trips…it was awesome. What an honor to do life at a young age with the one that you love. I truly felt like God's hand was all over our relationship.

So, Derrick and I were both excited to enter into the college world together (I'll give you a breakdown later on how this happened). We were both nervous and excited all at the same time. College was a whole new world for both of us. It was outside of our norm. We didn't know what to expect; we just knew that we were ready for whatever college life was going to bring.

In college, our relationship had many ups and downs. We broke up many times, but it was never for long. A day or two was all we could stand. It was challenging being without each other. We had our childish, silly moments of attitude, pride- fullness, and just getting caught up in the college world. We made friends who were "out there"—you know, party animals that liked to smoke, drink, and hang out all the time. The thing was, Derrick and I were never really like that. We had friends that were like that, but it wasn't really our cup of tea. We both hated smoke, and being around it made us sick. I wasn't a drinker, but I tried to drink around my friends just so I could "hang". My version of drinking was having a wine cooler or my favorite, Arbor Mist Wine. My friends often laughed at me because they would drink harder versions of liquor. I tried. It just wasn't my thing. I couldn't handle hard liquor very well, and it always made me sick to my stomach. I would complain to Derrick that I felt like I was having a heart attack! No joke! I felt like if I drank anything strong, it seemed as if it was doing something to my heart. I now realize that it was God shielding and protecting me. He never allowed me to get caught up in the hype of drinking. Though I did try, it was never my thing.

Derrick hated if I tried to drink. He knew that my friends were pros at it, and I was doing it just to fit in. He also knew that I couldn't handle alcohol very well, and he asked me not to do it around them. I felt like he was trying to "throw salt in my game". I thought he just didn't want me to hang out and have fun with my friends. In his own way, he was being very protective of "his girl". He knew my friends were kind of "out there," and I was "the good girl who came to college with her boyfriend of two years". As a matter of fact, I was the ONLY one in the group with that title. Needless to say, it was somewhat of a challenge for Derrick and I in college. At times, he didn't trust my friends, and I didn't trust his!

His friends, men of the Kappa Alpha Psi fraternity, were some "playboys". Yep, I said it! They were cool and fun, but I knew that they were players when it came to the ladies, so I didn't really trust them a lot with my husband. If I'm honest (and my husband knows this), many of them were flirting and hitting on me the entire time! So, if they flirted with me, their own fraternity brother's girlfriend, what were they trying to get him to do behind my back? I loved them, but trust was another issue. I know Derrick felt the same way about me and my girls, too.

Long story short, Derrick and I had to grow together in college. We had many moments where I felt like we were not going to make it. Being young, in college and committed to someone can be very challenging. You have to know without a shadow of a doubt that it's what you want. Our relationship was what we wanted. It's what was real to us. Yes, I had tons of guys trying to talk to me in college, and they knew I was in a relationship. Derrick had girls doing the same. We had to push past temptations and realize what was real. I would be lying if I told you that our relationship was perfect in college. It wasn't. But one thing was certain. We loved each other so much that it was hard for us to see the other with someone else. We were willing to fight for what was ours.

No matter how young or old you are, you have to be willing to fight for what you want out of life. Nothing comes easy.

After six years of dating and college were about to be under our belt, we knew it was time for the next level of our relationship to happen. Five years prior to graduating from college, the proposal was made. It was then that I accepted the sweetest, most innocent proposal from the man that I love. We knew we were destined to be together, but timing for marriage was everything to us. We wanted to be done with college and ready for the next phase of our lives together as one before we walked down the aisle.

We had finally arrived. Derrick graduated a semester before me. I had to do an extra semester because I had double-majored. Typically, with my double major, I was supposed to have graduated in about five years; however, I was determined to do it in four! There was no way I was going to let my husband graduate, and I would still have another year to go! No way! We started together, so we were going to finish together! So, I had a game plan that would allow me to finish my studies in four years. It wasn't the most logical, but it worked! My last semester of college, I was extremely burned out. I had taken no summers off, and I had done anywhere from 19-23 hours per semester! I worked hard! When I set my mind to do something, and I focus in on that thing, consider it done! Double-majoring and finishing in four years is probably one of the top 10 challenges that I faced in my life. It was very tedious, very time consuming. And the entire time that I was in school, I worked two jobs and still did all those hours! Not only that, I had to do two internships because of my double major. It was an extreme challenge! I remember calling my mom and crying. I was in my second to last semester doing internship number one. It was at that moment in my life that I felt like I needed a break because I simply couldn't do it anymore! No summers off and hours and hours of classes had finally taken their toll on me! I remember my mom telling me that I had worked so hard and had come this far. I simply could not stop and take a break right now. It would delay my graduation an entire semester. I would be closer to finishing in five years instead of four if I took a break at this stage in my life!

She was right. I had to find my second wind. I was in it to win it. Derrick was waiting on me to graduate so we could begin the next phase of our life together. I was one semester behind him. I was not about to add more to it. I was going to finish this thing so we could move on with our lives.

Derrick and I decided to get married on August 5th. Our wedding was going to be a couple of weeks before I started my last internship. I would be graduating in November and moving to Panama City, Florida at the end of December. We weren't going to have time nor money for a honeymoon. Yeah, we kind of overdid ourselves for the wedding, but at least we got it done! We overdid it so much that we had NO money for a honeymoon! I truly would do it so differently if I had to do it all over again! You know how we women can get. We want the fairytale wedding. We want to live the dream. We want to do it BIG! I wanted BIG, but I had no BIG money yet! Shoot, I hadn't even finished college. What was I thinking! Derrick was the only one that had a real job. What were we doing? Young. Immature. Ignorant. We just didn't know, but we learned! Yes, we learned!

Doing the popular thing doesn't mean it's the BEST thing.

Our wedding was beautiful. It was an extremely large wedding, but it was very lovely. We made sure we added ALL of our family and friends in there! That's no joke! I look back at it now, and I think…was there anyone that we didn't ask to be in the wedding! Again, we were young, immature and ignorant to quite a few things, but boy, we were ready to start learning…TOGETHER.

Chapter 2

The Essentials of a Healthy Marriage

The Essentials of a Healthy Marriage

After being with my husband for decades now, I must say that I have learned so much about him, about me, about marriage. It has shaped and molded me into the woman that I am today, so much so that I had to write this book.

My husband and I have counseled and continue to counsel so many couples. There are many people out there who desire marriage but don't understand how to maintain a healthy marriage.

I'm not saying that marriage has to be perfect, but it does need to be healthy. Exactly what do I mean by "healthy"?

If we studied the word healthy, we would learn several things. According to dictionary.com, healthy means "prosperous or sound". To have a healthy marriage means that your marriage is prospering daily; it means that it's pretty sound. In order for that to happen, both parties have to work diligently.

So, let's talk about what a man and woman should be doing daily in order to live the dream of having a healthy marriage. I'll break these down, but you'll see me really go into detail on some of them in other chapters. Let's get started.

Commitment. Commitment—involvement, a pledge, promise or obligation; the act of engaging oneself. Spouses in healthy marriages are committed to each other. They are dedicated to the partnership and maintain a long-term perspective so that short-term problems don't threaten the marriage ("What is a 'Healthy' Marriage," 2019).

When you are committed, you are engaging yourself. You act like you care. What's important to one is important to the other. You show up mentally, physically, emotionally, financially, etc., because you are committed to keeping your vows.

Derrick and I made a personal commitment to each other years ago while dating. We then took it to another level in our marriage. We hold each other accountable for our actions, our emotions, and our attitudes. We don't allow minor things to interfere with what God has given us.

You see, when you understand commitment, you won't easily run when things get hot in the kitchen. Because you are committed, you figure out ways to put out the fire TOGETHER. You figure out ways to turn down the heat TOGETHER. Why? Because you're both committed to the process of being married. Remember, I said earlier that when you are suitable, that means that you are "becoming". Every day, you should work on going to a deeper level of becoming the wife that you need to be.

There are times when you have to look at yourself and your marriage and figure out the areas in which you need to take your level of commitment up a notch or two. Are you committed to asking God to help you tame your tongue? Uh oh! That's a big one for us ladies because you know we always have a LOT to say! I'll talk more on that later. Are you committed to looking at your weaknesses and working on being better? Are you committed to taking your honor and respect for your husband to another level? Are you committed to submitting to your husband more? Now that word seems like a curse word to many women! Submit. Submit. Submit. It makes them think that they are a slave to a man. I beg to differ. Submitting is not slave mentality when it comes to marriage. When you don't understand submission, it's hard to commit to doing it, but I want to bring some truth to that in this book. We'll also talk about that more in a later chapter.

Ladies, in a nutshell, we have to look at our marriage and figure out how we can commit more of ourselves to it daily. Are you going through the motions of being married and not really LIVING the married life? Living the married life brings excitement, joy, and peace daily. Going through the motions of being married creates a void that's hard to explain, but you know it's there. That's because something is missing. Commitment in some area or another is missing. Somebody is not showing up daily and working their position. They're just going through the motions and checking the box in order to say that at least they showed up. Showing up is not necessarily showing commitment! When you show up, you have to be present. Be present daily. Do your job daily. Commit yourself daily.

Otherwise, you're not really living the dream. You're sleepwalking and praying that things will be better soon. Commitment makes you show up and live the dream! Commitment makes you and everyone around you better. Commitment and dedication make your dream your reality. It's time to take your commitment to another level.

"Love is an unconditional commitment to an imperfect person. To love somebody isn't just a strong feeling. It is a decision, a judgement, and a promise." — Paulo Coelho

Finding rhythm in a relationship is the biggest challenge for a couple. It's easy to fall in love, once you've found someone. (Prior to the relationship, the finding someone is indeed the hardest part!) It's easy to say, "I love you," once you've shared some special moments with a boyfriend or girlfriend.

But what about that consistency we all crave, which comes only from true commitment? That's a lot harder but absolutely possible. Commitment begins with desire. Each person has to want it and be willing to sacrifice for the other. It takes shifting the way we view ourselves and giving up something in order to give to someone else. The thing is, it's not as hard as you might think.

Marriage is the covenant that's meant to last a lifetime. It's a commitment that you make for a lifetime. It's a lifestyle of being committed. It's not being committed only when the times are good. You have to have a lifestyle of commitment, no matter what comes your way.

So, I want to give you five keys to being and staying committed in your marriage:

1. Positive Experiences

A great confidence and commitment builder in a relationship is shared, positive experiences with the person you love (Connors, 2017). You have to be intentional about having as many positive experiences in your marriage as you can have. You have to be intentional in creating positive atmospheres, which in turn will evoke the positive experiences that you want to have.

I tell my husband all the time that he is an atmosphere creator for our house. He is the head of our home. How he comes into the house can change the atmosphere for good or for bad. I'll give you an example. The kids and I are playing, laughing and joking, having a really good family fun time while we wait for dad to come home from work. Dad finally makes it in, and he's frowning, has an attitude, doesn't want to really talk to anyone and wants everyone to chill out and not be loud. Well, you just came in and shattered our atmosphere filled with positivity, Sir! Yep, you did that! Now the kids are looking like what in the world is wrong with Daddy? They want to know why you're being mean, why you're not laughing and joking with the family. Why does the house now have to go into this gloomy mode because you're not embracing our positivity, simply because you had a bad day at work, or you're tired and don't want to do anything, or you're not in a happy mood?

My husband soon realized the power that he had with his presence in the home. He understood that he could make it good, or he could totally destroy what we had going on with negativity. But get this ladies—it's not just with the man. It's with us, too. If we want to be more committed to having positive experiences, then we have to be committed to watching our attitudes, to watching our body language, to watching how we care for and love our spouses. We have to be committed to next-level greatness in our marriage! This type of commitment enhances the longevity of our marriage.

We have to learn to take the negative, funny things and turn them into positive experiences. We can now laugh, joke, and teach about how we come in and shift the atmosphere with our attitudes. We study it, realize what we are doing, and we commit to going to another level of being better. We take the negative, turn it into positive experiences, and live through the memories and build toward new experiences. That's all a part of being committed.

"Love is not maximum emotion. Love is maximum commitment." — Sinclair B. Ferguson

2. Going "All In" in Thoughts, Words, and Actions

Essentially, this is the strategy I aim to live by each day. I've heard it said, "You're here. You're present. So be present. Work hard!" Exactly. Relationships take work! You have to show up for "work" daily with the mindset that you're all in. You're in it to win it. There's no let up. There's no let down. You're aiming to please, and you're going to do just that! It all starts with the mindset. How you think, so shall you be! How you think, so shall you do! How you think, so shall you become! There will be easy, seamless days, but there will also be conflict and struggle! You have to be ready to take on and handle it all with the mindset that you're ALL IN!

What I'm getting at is value your time with your partner. Value those moments (Connors, 2017). The moments we share with the people we love are so precious. Go "all in". Think about what will make your husband happy. Think about ways to improve your relationship, fun things to do, or chores that will help ease his burden. In other words, express your love and tell your husband that you care. Most importantly, SHOW that you care. Actions will always speak louder than words, but that doesn't mean words and thoughts don't matter. Those are what contribute to your actions. So, go ahead—get your man something special. Put on absolutely nothing and welcome him into your "home"! Oh yeah…you just wait till we get to the sex chapter! ☺ Tell him you love him. Let him know that he's the most important person in your life. You're all in! Nothing is going to stop your marriage from being fabulous because you're focused on thinking, saying and doing the right things!

3. Eliminating Distractions and Temptations

Another key to staying committed to your marriage is that you have to eliminate distractions and temptations! That guy who checked you out and asked for your number at work? Forget it. Working on your job more than you work on your marriage…. Staying on your phone/social media and rarely showing attention to your man, or when you're supposed to be paying attention to him, you're paying more attention to your phone than anything, vices, temptations, minor distractions—these are the things that tear relationships apart (Connors, 2017). And most of the time, it's not exactly the big-bang approach. It's more the slow, gradual, pernicious path to destruction.

To be faithful and committed, you have to eliminate the temptations, like too much perusing on Facebook or letting your mind wander too much in social settings. We're all vulnerable to letting our minds and eyes wander. Let's face it—there are tons of attractive men and women out in the world. That doesn't mean they can have our attention, especially if we're committed to someone in a covenant called marriage! Things like alcohol, emotionally-charged occasions, and fatigue can all contribute to putting us in a position where we're weak.

To have a successful marriage, you have to understand when you're allowing distractions to get the best of you. Distractions can come in many forms. Knowledge is recognizing what form it's in. Wisdom is doing something about what you recognize.

4. A Willingness to Understand Things from Your Husband's Point of View

This is a very strong element to being committed to having a healthy marriage. We're always going to see things through our own experiences first. That's a fact of life. But what separates great relationships from mediocre ones is a willingness to understand your husband's needs, wants, and point of view. You have to throw your ego out the window and understand where he is coming from (Connors, 2017).

The problem with women a lot of times is that we always think we're right. We always think we have things figured out. What I've learned over the years is that I need to stop acting like it's my way or the highway. I had to become more intentional in hearing how my husband felt, and not only did I listen to him, I had to change my perspective on how I heard him. You see, being heard for men or being listened to is a way that we as women can honor and show respect. Respect is HUGE for men! I'll talk about that more later, but hearing and listening to your husband is a great way for you to respect him. I think about all the times that I merely only "heard" my husband, but because I wasn't listening to him, I missed the point of what he was saying. You know, ladies…how we can be scrolling on social media at the time that we're supposed to be listening. That means that we haven't given our spouses our full attention because we're somewhat distracted by seeing what everyone else is doing. We have to learn to keep the main thing…THE MAIN THING! Or, when the kids are pulling on you during the time that you and your husband are supposed to be sharing and talking about something really important. Listen, one of the most important things that you can do is to listen to him. Listen to what he says, but also listen to what he isn't saying. What he "isn't saying" is evident if you are simply paying attention to him!

Part of your commitment to your husband is satisfying a need for him. Be a great listener. Do something kind. Always express a genuine interest in understanding his point of view! That's one of the ways that you can honor and respect him.

5. What Matters Most

Here's a question for you. Do you know what matters most to your husband? What does he desire from you the most? What would make him feel like the king in your kingdom? How can you honor and respect him more?

You see, when you learn what matters most to your husband, you will make a point of seeing that he gets it. That's right—you care about how he feels. You want him to feel like THE man, and you're willing to do whatever you need to do to make him feel like just that!

One of the things that I've learned is that many women don't really know what matters the most to their husbands. They don't understand how to speak his language back to him. Wisdom is telling me to tell you right now…find out what that is! Find out what he desires the most from you as his wife. For some, that may be attention, time, more sex, or support. Whatever it is, do your best to go to the next level in fulfilling that desire, even when you don't feel like it!

In the end, focusing on the things that matters most to each of you will change the dynamics of your marriage from good to great!

Let's make a point in making sure the following elements are there:

Satisfaction. In healthy marriages, both individuals need to be satisfied. About 90% of married people say they are satisfied with their marriage. This is not because their marriages are void of problems, but rather because both spouses are committed to persevering through both good and difficult situations ("What is a 'Healthy' Marriage," 2019).

Good Communication. Using clear communication to solve problems is one of the strongest indicators of healthy relationships ("What is a 'Healthy' Marriage," 2019). Now this is a weak point for many marriages, so I'm going to dedicate an entire chapter on talking about this topic!

Effective Conflict Resolution. Individuals who have established healthy marriages are able to resolve conflict effectively. Spouses who effectively overcome stress and conflict are able to avoid criticism, contempt, and defensiveness from their marriages ("What is a 'Healthy' Marriage," 2019). Ask yourself, on a level of 1-10, how do you rate how the two of you handle conflict?

Lack of Violence and Abuse. In healthy marriages, spouses never use aggression or violence to gain control over each other. This includes, but is not limited to, verbal, physical, emotional, and sexual abuse. They also never abuse or mistreat their children ("What is a 'Healthy' Marriage," 2019).

Fidelity or Faithfulness. In healthy marriages, spouses are sexually and emotionally faithful to each other. On the other hand, infidelity is one of the most common causes of divorce ("What is a 'Healthy' Marriage," 2019). Sexual faithfulness in marriage includes more than just our bodies. It also includes our eyes, mind, heart, and soul (Becker, 2019). When we devote our minds to sexual fantasies about another person, we sacrifice sexual faithfulness to our spouse. When we offer moments of emotional intimacy to another, we also sacrifice sexual faithfulness to our spouse. Guard your sexuality daily and devote it entirely to your spouse. Sexual faithfulness requires self-discipline and an awareness of the consequences. Refuse to put anything in front of your eyes, body, or heart that would compromise your faithfulness to your husband.

Intimacy and Emotional Support. Spouses who are intimate, emotionally supportive, trusting, and caring have healthy marriages ("What is a 'Healthy' Marriage," 2019).

Friendship and Spending Time Together. In healthy marriages, spouses act like best friends and spend quality time together. Couples often have different hobbies, but a key indicator of a healthy marriage is that couples enjoy each other's company and have a respect for one another ("What is a 'Healthy' Marriage," 2019).

Commitment to Children. Spouses who are both committed to their children tend to enjoy more enriching marriages ("What is a 'Healthy' Marriage," 2019).

Duration and Legal Status. Spouses in healthy marriages believe in the permanence of their relationship. They are more likely to stay together when faced with difficult life circumstances ("What is a 'Healthy' Marriage," 2019).

Love/Commitment. At its core, love is a decision to be committed to another person. It is far more than a fleeting emotion as portrayed on television, the big screen, and romance novels. Feelings come and go, but a true decision to be committed lasts forever, and that is what defines true love. It is a decision to be committed through the ups and the downs, the good and the bad. When things are going well, commitment is easy. But true love is displayed by remaining committed even through the trials of life.

Humility. We all have weaknesses, and relationships always reveal these faults quicker than anything else on earth. An essential building block of a healthy marriage is the ability to admit that you are not perfect, that you will make mistakes, and that you will need forgiveness (Becker, 2019). Holding an attitude of superiority over your husband will bring about resentment and will prevent your relationship from moving forward (Becker, 2019). If you struggle in this area, grab a pencil and quickly write down three things that your husband does better than you. That simple exercise should help you stay humble. Repeat as often as necessary.

Patience/Forgiveness. Because no one is perfect, patience and forgiveness will always be required in a marriage relationship. Successful partners learn to show unending patience and forgiveness to their spouse. They humbly admit their own faults and do not expect perfection from the other (Becker, 2019). They do not bring up past errors in an effort to hold their partner hostage, and they do not seek to get revenge when mistakes occur. If you are holding on to a past hurt from your husband, it's time that you forgive him. It will set your heart and relationship free.

Time. Relationships don't work without time investment. Never have, never will. Any successful relationship requires intentional, quality time together. And quality time rarely happens when quantity time is absent. The relationship with your spouse should be the most intimate and deep relationship you have (Becker, 2019). Therefore, it is going to require more time than any other relationship. If possible, set aside time each day for your spouse. You have to be intentional about having date nights, pillow talk sessions, walks in the park or neighborhood, bike rides, or spa days. This is definitely an area that I want to take to another level in my marriage. At one point in our lives, my husband and I got so consumed in our "miracle babies" that all of our date nights turned into family nights. We were just so happy to have children that we didn't know what else to do! Let's just say having kids was quite a challenge for us. Once we realized that we weren't really having our time together, we became more intentional in having our "we time" together. I challenge you to evaluate your time together. How are you spending it? Are you doing enough? Do you feel like it needs to go to another level? If so, what's your plan for doing it? Right now, this is just us thinking together, but thoughts are merely fantasies if you never take action behind them. Remember that.

Honesty and Trust. Honesty and trust become the foundation for everything healthy in a marriage. But unlike most of the other essentials on this list, trust takes time. You can become selfless, committed, or patient in a moment, but trust always takes time. Trust is only built after weeks, months, and years of being who you say you are and doing what you say you'll do. It takes time, so start now…and if you need to rebuild trust in your relationship, you'll need to work even harder (Becker, 2019).. Once trust has been broken, there's this void in the marriage that's hard to fill. The only way for it to disappear is you have to put in much WORK, especially if you're the one that's the cause for the trust to be lost. That person has to be humble enough to say and know that they are the reason that "the house", your marriage, is on shaky ground. When you are committed, you will do everything to keep honesty and trust a priority in your marriage.

Communication. Successful marriage partners communicate as much as possible. They certainly discuss kids' schedules, grocery lists, utility bills, etc. But they don't stop there. They also communicate hopes, dreams, fears, and anxieties. They don't just discuss the changes that are taking place in the kids' lives; they also discuss the changes that are taking place in their own hearts and souls. This essential key cannot be overlooked because honest, forthright communication becomes the foundation for so many other things on this list: commitment, patience, and trust…just to name a few (Becker, 2019). Communication is extremely important, and is one of the number-one reasons why marriages fail. That's why I have to dedicate a whole chapter to this topic. We'll go into more details later.

Selflessness. Although it will never show up on any survey, more marriages are broken up by selfishness than any other reason. Surveys blame it on finances, lack of commitment, infidelity, or incompatibility, but the root cause for most of these reasons is selfishness. PRIDE IS A KILLER! A selfish person is committed only to himself or herself, shows little patience, and never learns how to be a successful spouse. Give your hopes, dreams, and life to your spouse and begin to live life together (Becker, 2019). A selfish marriage never lasts. That's why every single day, you have to make sure that your husband's concerns are your concerns. The same goes for the husband. The husband has to make his wife's concerns his concerns. When you work together at walking in selflessness, nothing will be able to stop what you two can do together! Don't allow pride to kill your marriage! Stay humble and committed. When you do that, you always WIN!

This is a simple call to value our marriages. We want, need, and desire healthy marriages; therefore, spouses should treat each other with great care and invest into their marriages daily. Accomplishing the items listed above will always require nearly every bit of YOU…but it is so worth it. After all, a successful marriage is far more valuable than most of the temporal things we chase after in our lives. And a successful marriage will always last longer. It's time to focus on the main thing. Keep the main thing, the main thing. You'll always come out victorious!

Chapter 3

Dealing with YOU

Dealing with YOU

This is where it gets deep. This is where you begin to look at you, not him anymore. It's all about you.

In essence, when you're married and have issues, it's easy to point out all of the horrible things that your spouse is doing. Yeah, there's a whole list for that! And it's easy to make yourself look like the saint in the process.

Over the years, I've learned a simple lesson.

Okay, so this is oftentimes a hard lesson to learn and a hard habit to grasp. In life, we become

---

When you change, everything around you changes.

---

so stuck in our ways that changing is a challenge.

So, where do I go with this? I'll give you ME for an example.

As you already know, seeing healthy marriages for me was not common. My mom and dad's marriage wasn't the best, but I knew that they loved each other. They still do today, even though they are not together. They have an agape kind of love for one another, which is a good thing. Afterall, they did have four kids together. Nevertheless, watching them as I grew up allowed me to develop certain mindsets and characteristics. For example, I knew that I wanted commitment, but I didn't want to commit to anyone who was like my daddy. I know it's sad, but it's true. I didn't want a man who had eyes for other women. I knew I was going to be really selfish in that area…and with every right! My husband had NO grounds to be looking and making advances toward other women! It had to be all about me! I didn't want the arguing. I didn't want the strife.

I didn't want the abuse. I simply wanted to be happy with the man of my dreams. I soon learned that I had "daddy issues". Yes, major ones! I was insecure about men. I had trust issues. When we got together, would he be faithful to me? Would he love me unconditionally? Would he do everything in his power to make me happy and to make sure that I was well taken care of? I was insecure in that area. Could I trust someone with my heart? I only wanted to be loved and cherished as a queen. I wanted the fairytale depiction of what marriage looked like. I learned that it really doesn't exist. Even if you have a really good marriage, you're still going to have bumps in the road. It's how you deal with those bumps that matters.

When my husband and I first started dating, I laid down the law! Well, I just told him my expectations and goals. I told him what was NOT going to happen when we started dating. In essence, I kind of poured out my insecurities in a more authoritative way. Hmm…yeah. That's exactly what I did!

You see, I never wanted to waste my time with any man. I always dated with a purpose. I told my husband (then boyfriend) that I was not the kind of girl that would just sleep around with boys. If he was going to date me, he had to understand that he was going to date a girl with purpose and destiny attached to her heart and mind. I let him know that if he was serious, it had to be about me and nobody else because I was NOT about games! I look back now and chuckle at myself a little bit. It's funny how I always knew what I wanted. Once my mind was focused on reaching a goal, nothing could stop me from reaching it but ME. I've always been that way. I brought that mindset into our relationship.

But, let's get back to one of my issues—the daddy issues that caused me to have trust issues with men. I was always very attentive. I noticed everything. Even at a young age, I remember having a very strong gift of discerning spirits. I could pick up on people's emotions, actions that were not visible to the human eyes but only the spiritual eyes, as well as people's thoughts at times. Yeah, I know that's weird at such a young age, but I've always been like that. It's part of my calling as a prophet of God, but that's a book for another day.

As a teenager, I was very tomboyish. I was very athletic. I played numerous sports, but my main thing was basketball. My husband as well. When we were dating, our dates would include shooting ball together. Weird, I know, but we definitely had a *Love and Basketball* kind of relationship. We enjoyed those times together as we were able to do what we both loved all the time while spending time together. Because my husband was a star athlete in football, he was pretty popular in school. He wasn't a loud and obnoxious guy. He was pretty humble, yet cool all at the same time. He was my guy, and everybody knew it. If they didn't, I would let them know really quickly all about it!

I would notice the sly smiles of some girls, and I knew they were up to no good. Try it! Let's see how far that would get you! Listen, I was the only girl out of with five brothers. I grew up fighting. I practiced fighting and wrestling all the time at home with the fellows, so I wasn't afraid to pop somebody in the mouth! I'm being real in this book, but I do want to say this…THANK GOD FOR DELIVERANCE! I'm not as feisty as I used to be. Now I engage and fight spiritual battles and not physical ones. Back then, I wasn't afraid to fight! I would challenge anyone that looked at my husband (then boyfriend) a certain way.

Why? It all goes back to my insecurities; however, at the same time, I could pick up on a lot of things that were going on by the Spirit, and I didn't even know that was what it was until years later.

Trust issues, insecurities, and fears are some of the baggage that women have in a relationship. As a young girl, I was afraid of being cheated on. I was insecure. Was I pretty enough? Sexy enough? Was I enough? You see, growing up, I don't remember a time that my daddy told me that I was pretty. I think back over my life, and I can honestly say I don't recall ever hearing that from my dad. I would have loved to hear it! I had so many insecurities growing up! Many of my family on my mom's side has gaps in their teeth. I was one of those ones growing up that inherited the "gap tooth". I remember looking in the mirror as a young girl and covering the space between my two front teeth with my finger. I would then smile to see how pretty I was without the gap. I thought to myself that I would look a whole lot prettier if I didn't have this gap in between my two front teeth. My parents never got me braces as a child. I purposed in my heart that when I got older, I was going to buy me some braces to correct my teeth. I didn't want this inheritance! Why was I the one with the gap? I didn't smile a lot. Or if I did, I would cover my mouth or give a big smile without showing my teeth. That was just one of my insecurities. When I got older, I did exactly as I had planned. Those teeth got fixed!

Things like that made me wonder if I was pretty enough for Derrick. Would he desire someone else with a prettier smile? I would sometimes look at him and get the feeling that the answer was yes. On the inside, those thoughts made me feel really bad. Insecure thoughts are only there to bring you to a low place. It's always a trick of the enemy (the devil himself). He wants us to be insecure about who we are. He wants us to feel bad, to feel down, to feel like we're not enough.

If you don't control your thoughts, your thoughts will control you. They'll consume you. Either you'll go in a positive direction or to a very low place. Your thoughts are always subject to your control.

If you change your thinking, you change your life. Over the years of us dating, my husband and I had a few bumps in the road. You know…the kind of bumps that make you not even want to stay. We broke up several times, but we could never end up staying apart from one another. We knew deep down within that we were destined to be together.

As we were going along the journey, I began to realize a few things about myself. I guess you can call it maturity. As the years rolled by, I was beginning to mature in many areas. Being the only girl in the family, I'll admit I was a little spoiled. I was used to getting things my way, or at least I would figure out a way to get things my way. Not only was I spoiled, but I had an attitude problem when I couldn't get things my way. Also, when something was on my mind, I just said it. I didn't care how anyone felt about it. I knew I was right the majority of the time. So, it made it easier for me to say things without caring how anyone felt about it. The truth hurts. Oh well, I thought. Okay, so I know that's not right. Well, let's just say I figured it out later. My husband let me know one day. He said, "Babe, you're probably 90% right most of the time, but the way you present yourself is all wrong. When you do that, it's hard for anyone to receive from you." Wait, Sir. You're saying that I'm right, but you won't receive it because my presentation is wrong?? Hmm…let me meditate on that for a second.

I began to pay more attention to the things I said and how I said them. I paid attention to the responses from others. I began to make slight changes here and there just to see if it made a difference. I must admit…Derrick was right. How I presented myself made a big deal in the reception of others. I had to ask God to give me better ways of saying and doing things. I wanted to speak truth, but I had to learn how to speak the truth in love. Not only that, I also had an issue where I would cut you off from speaking just so I could get my point across because I felt like what you were saying wasn't right, so I had to cut you off in order to let you know that you weren't right. I had to learn to listen and hear what people were saying to me. I had to learn how to value my husband's feelings and not just think that it was my way or the highway.

My way or the highway…yeah, unfortunately, that's how I was thinking a lot of times, but it's funny that I didn't recognize it until years later. As I stated earlier, I always knew what I wanted. I am very strong-minded, very strong-willed. I had to realize that how I was coming off to people, including my husband, wasn't necessarily right. You see, it's okay to be strong-minded. It's okay to know what you want out of life, but what's not okay is using your "strong will/strong mind" to strong arm people. It's almost like bullying. Wow. That just hit me. It's almost like bullying but without the physical aggression. It's all mental. I had to learn how to leverage being a strong-minded woman. I had to learn how to be gentler and kinder. I had to learn how to listen. I had to learn how to hear the words that my husband or anyone else was saying to me. I had a wall up. I was afraid of being hurt. I was afraid of rejection. I was afraid of not living the dream.

Leveraging being so strong-minded and purpose-driven was not as easy as I thought it would be. You see, my husband and I grew up totally differently. I grew up spoiled to a certain extent, and he grew up in a lot of lack. I grew up being trained mentally and physically on how to be a strong girl, a fighter, a winner, a woman of purpose and destiny, and my husband grew up not really understanding what it meant to be a strong man that can stand up and take care of things. I'll admit. That sometimes bothered me…a lot.

I was always very assertive. I liked to make a decision and follow through with that decision. I wanted my husband to be the same way, and when he wasn't, sometimes an argument would arise. I just needed him to make a decision. Tell me where we're going to dinner. Tell me what you feel like doing. Tell me your ideas. Just tell me. It was frustrating for me sometimes when he would go back and forth with a decision. Because of that, sometimes my response would make him feel disrespected and dishonored. Remember, I always just said things. How it came out…well, I'd think about that later. For now, I just needed to say it. Many times, my response would come out in a frustrating way. I never wanted my husband to feel less than; I just simply wanted him to lead. I wanted him to be assertive. I wanted him to know without a doubt what we were doing.

I had to learn how to talk to my husband. I had to learn how to share my feelings. I had to help him become the man that he needed to be, and all the while, he had to help me evolve into the woman that I knew I could be. We had to grow with each other. We had to have patience and understanding with one another.

Many women don't realize it, but we have the power to raise a man up into kingship or the

Watch your words. They have the power to build or demolish. What you say could be the beginning or the end of something. The power of life and death lies within your tongue.

power to tear him down into a pit. Our words are powerful. It's not just what we say; I've learned over the years that it's also how we say it.

I had to learn to build my husband up. I had to empower him. I wanted him to feel like the king in our palace. I wanted him to know that he means the world to me, that I would do anything for him. That included humbling myself when it came to the way I communicated. You see, men don't want to stay in the house with a nagging wife, a wife that acts more like a mother than a wife, or a wife that makes them feel like less of a man. The Bible says men would prefer to sit on the rooftop of a house rather than be in the house with that type of woman (Proverbs 21:9).

Women are emotional beings. We share our feelings constantly. We always want to talk, and what we don't realize is that men feel like our "talk" is more nagging than anything. They don't want you to be their mother. They want you to be their wife. There were so many things that bothered me about my husband, and for some reason, I felt a need to explain that to him. The way that it was explained may have come across wrong. Men are very sensitive. Any "little" thing in our eyes can come across as a thing of "disrespect" in their eyes. I've learned over the years that what men desire the most is R-E-S-P-E-C-T. Yep, that's it. They want to feel respected more than anything. Women…well, let's just say we want to feel loved more than anything.

So now the question was how do I respect my husband while still pushing him to another level of excellence and greatness in our marriage? Remember, I am one who was always very blunt with my conversations. Black and white. There were rarely any gray areas for me. So this was going to be new for me, but I was willing to try.

If you speak to the King, you'll get kingly results. If you speak to the fool, you'll get foolish results.

I've heard it said before that if you talk to the man like he's a king, you'll get a kingly response, but if you talk to him like he's a fool, then you'll get a foolish response. Inside of every man is a king and a fool. Which one do you want to do marriage with? Whatever your response is, your actions have to back it up. That means you have to watch the way you talk to your man, even when he has ticked you off beyond measure! Yep, humbling I know, but it's a must. Remember, the power of life and death is in the tongue. Are you spitting life, or are you spitting death (unintentionally)? You have the power to build a man up or tear him all the way down. Choose this day which one you prefer to do.

My husband and I were just having this conversation about a couple that's very dear to us. He was trying to give him godly counsel in regards to their marriage. This comes very naturally to us as we do this all the time. This one was somewhat different. As the young man began to talk to my husband, he began to tell him how "less of a man" he felt. He talked about the financial problems that he and his wife were having. He then began to describe how she talks to him in the midst of all of their frustrations. He said he'd never been called so many SOBs in all of his life. He was told how he wasn't being a man, a provider, etc. In essence, his wife was pulling out all of the "negative" qualities about him in the midst of them going through a very difficult trial. He was in a very low place. He was a man of God, a minister. He was in a backslidden condition, not really doing church, God or family because the frustrations of life were just a bit too much in this season of his life. He began to look at church folks as hypocritical. His wife was still in church and going consistently, but he couldn't see how she was still going and talking to him the way that she was talking to him. Even with others in the church as well, he felt like he was getting similar responses from them, but of course, not as bad as from his wife. All in all, he was experiencing hurt in his marriage and hurt from the church as well. Now, we know that there are two sides to every story, but in this moment, I want you to hear what the man is saying about his wife. Regardless of what was going on, obviously the problems have existed for some time now, and I'm sure the story is a lot deeper; however, what we are considering is how the man is feeling through it all.

You see, we women are truly emotional, but men have feelings, too. They may not express them as we would, but they certainly feel wounded when we come at them wrong. Let's take this person for example. I'll just call him Charles so that the real name isn't exposed. Charles knows that he and his wife have issues. He knows the struggle is real, but Charles isn't focusing on the main issues in his marriage. His focus is on how he feels disrespected and less of a man in his own marriage, regardless of whatever else is going on.

That's it, ladies. When a man feels disrespected, he feels at a loss in his marriage. Respect is everything. How you talk to him is everything. How you treat him is everything. If you treat him like a fool, he's going to feel like a fool while being with you. If you treat him like a king, he's going to feel like a king while being with you. How are you treating your man?

My husband and I can relate. We were going through some financial burdens a few times in our lives. It was extremely difficult and extremely challenging for us. We weren't sure how we'd make it, but we knew we could. We simply could not give up throughout the process.

I remember it like yesterday. We both had finished college and were ready to move to a new state, starting a new adventure. I had accepted a teaching job in Panama City, Florida. It was a two for one deal. They would hire me and give my husband a position, simply because I said, "Yes" (you can read more details of this story in my book *Faith in a Barren Land*). So, long story short…it was a LIE. They hired me, but failed to give my husband the position they had promised him. That left us struggling to find a job for my husband. It became extremely frustrating at times. There were moments when I could do nothing but cry. No matter what, it seemed as though we could never have enough to pay bills. We were in our *"pork and beans and weenies season"* while all the while praying and wishing that our *"steak and potato season"* would come soon.

I will say that the struggle was real, but what was more real was our relationship. Our marriage was everything. I remember my husband working three jobs at a time just to try and make the ends meet. They were three very odd jobs that still didn't pay enough to cover what we needed, but I remember my husband doing what he had to do until something better came along. I must say, it took a minute for that something better to come; however, we continued to work with what we had until we could get what we wanted.

How did I respond to my husband during those most challenging financial times of our lives? Well, I'm glad you asked! You see, finances are something that can absolutely tear a marriage apart. In this marriage right here, WE REFUSED TO LET THAT HAPPEN!

So, let's talk about it. How did we overcome the financial slump? How did I respond to my husband during one of the most difficult challenges of our marriage?

My husband could tell you better than I can. I'm sure he will in his chapter of this book. Let me tell you from my end. I NEVER once got mad or frustrated at my husband. I never once made him feel less of a man for not being able to provide in the way that our household needed. We never had arguments about finances in the hardest time of our lives. Instead, we chose to never let finances come between what God gave us with each other. Shoot, I didn't marry him for money! Listen, we were a couple of young, naïve kids straight out of college. We didn't have a lot of money when we married. So money didn't unite us, and money sure wasn't going to break us apart!

I made a decision that no matter what, I was going to encourage my husband. I was going to empower him to do and to be all that God wanted him to be. We may have been struggling, but without a doubt, I knew that was only for a season. We simply had to endure as good soldiers. This was a test for us. Being young and married, we were determined to pass the test and get over this slump! This slump was NOT going to get over on us! We were determined and destined to win…TOGETHER!

My husband and I have counseled a lot of married couples in regards to financial distress. Here's a fact, a hard truth: many couples can't make it pass it. They don't know how. The frustration is just too heavy. There is a great divide, such a divide that there's no coming back, and it results in a divorce. I think it's so sad to see marriages fall to the wayside simply because of finances, so much so that I have an entire chapter devoted to it! Oh yeah. We're going to talk about finances because it can become a monster of division within marriages!

So, with that being said, let's get back to DEALING WITH ME! We'll talk more on finances in just a bit.

Sometimes, you have to look in the mirror at the woman you are and see the woman that you can become. Stare at the woman in the mirror. Ask her to change her ways. Ask her to become better, do better and be better for those around her.

I had to become the woman that I wanted to see. That insecure little girl with daddy issues had to grow up. That little girl that didn't think she was pretty had to learn to see past her flaws and recognize her beauty regardless of who confirmed it or not. The woman with the trust issues had to learn to be vulnerable. The woman with the feisty words had to allow the Lord to tame her tongue. The little girl simply had to grow up.

To live the fairytale life, to live the dream, I had to become. The becoming never stops. Every day is a process of becoming. Every day is a process of getting better, wiser, and stronger. Every day is a new process for having more in life and more in my marriage. Every day, I choose to look at myself in the mirror and recognize my flaws, see my weaknesses, and do better. If I want better, then I have to be better. If I want change, then I have to change. If I want more, then I have to become more. It all starts with the woman in the mirror. It all starts with her making a decision to change her actions. It starts with recognizing that she doesn't have it all together like she thought. Truth is, it's not about your husband. It's about you. What are you willing to do to help your marriage become better? When you change, everything around you changes. You simply have to make the decision. I made it. As a matter of fact, I make it every day of my life. Will you join me on the course to being the best wife that you can possibly be? It's a challenge that I give myself daily. It's a challenge that I accept daily. Every day is not peaches and cream. Most days are better than others. I may still have a "moment" every now and then, but those aren't often. I make sure of that. I can honestly say that my husband and I have a great marriage. Once we figured out that it all starts with us as individuals, we both purposed in our hearts to be the best that we can be as individuals so that in our marriage, we can be the best husband and wife that we can be to each other.

It's really that simple, but it's really that challenging as well. You simply have to get over your ego. Once you do that, it's uphill from there. Be encouraged. It's not about him. Focus on YOU, and everything around you will change. I'm a living witness to that!

Chapter 4

Dealing with HIM

Dealing with HIM

I remember it like it was yesterday. My mom had made a decision to transfer me from one school to another. I was no longer going to attend school in Jackson, Alabama. She was transferring me to my new school, Grove Hill Elementary School in Grove Hill, Alabama. I didn't know what to expect. I had spent my entire kindergarten year in Jackson. Would I be able to make new friends? Would they like me? Would the teachers be nice? I had so many questions, but being so young, I didn't know how to ask them. I was somewhat quiet at a young age. Notice I said "young age". I kind of grew out of that as the years went along.

My first day of school in Grove Hill was nice. I remember walking into the class and seeing all the kids, the colorful decorations of the environment, and my teacher who seemed really nice. She introduced me to the class. I looked around at all the smiles from the kids. There was one in particular that I noticed far more than all the others.

He was beautiful to me, inside and out. I noticed there was something different about this young man. I wasn't quite sure what it was, but I knew that I liked it. It was a weird feeling because at the tender age of six, I knew absolutely nothing about liking boys. As a matter of fact, I was a tomboy myself. Why was I feeling this way? What were those feelings? I didn't quite understand them at so young of an age, but I knew that when I saw this young man, there was something about him that made my heart flutter. He gave me butterflies in first grade. Who does that?

I soon learned that his name was Derrick and that he lived in the area that my grandmother lived. He was really nice, and he was kind of shy, too. We would often look at each other and turn our eyes quickly when we realized that the other one was looking. It was totally cute now that I think about it!

Derrick had caramel skin, beautiful lips, a cute smile, and what I loved most…those bowed legs! I just love my bow-legged man! Yessss! But wait…he wasn't my man yet, so let me get y'all to the point of him being just that.

Derrick loved to play with me on the playground. We flirted a lot from the first grade on until we started dating in high school. I remember most of the time, each year, we had some of the same classes together. I'll never forget that one time in fourth grade in Mrs. Lanier's class. We were doing circle reading time. During this time, you could pick someone to be your partner and read with you. Derrick got to choose who his partner was going to be. I knew he would choose me! Wait for it…wait for it…. That joker chose to read with another girl!!! Wait…hold on…did you just do what I think you did? I was soooooo angry! I remember being angry the entire day. As a matter of fact, I was mad at him for that entire week!

It was the first time that I felt rejected in a relationship with someone else. I know you're thinking, *"Girl you were in 4th grade and not even in a relationship!"* Oh, I know, but I can't help how I felt. Remember, I'm the girl with the daddy issues, the trust issues, and I didn't know I had those issues at that time because I was simply too young for all of that, but I had them. Derrick and I were not in a relationship. We were too young for that. All I knew was that I had feelings that I didn't really know I had for a young boy who perhaps didn't even like me. At least at that moment I didn't think he liked me.

I was wrong. He had a huge crush on me. I found it out later, but I already knew because of the way we played and talked and interacted with one another. There was a very strong chemistry that we had together. Of course, at that age, we didn't know what to call it, but that's what it was and is today—CHEMISTRY.

My grandmother's house became my most favorite place in the world to visit. Not just because she was awesome and my favorite grandmother of the two that I had, but also because I knew Derrick was right around the corner from her. I would visit her to spend time with her, eat her most awesome cooking and hopefully get a chance to see my friend from school. He would sometimes come from "around the mountain" to play with us. Whenever he did, it made my whole day!

I even loved those times that we would ride the bus to grandmother's house instead of home. I loved it because Derrick was on that bus. I got to see him, perhaps even sit on the seat with him or even close to him. I don't remember us ever sitting on the seat together because we were both so shy at that age, but we would sit close to each other. I remember Derrick's sister, Wanda, telling us that she knew we liked each other and that we needed to start sitting together and talking to one another. I would look at her and smile shyly and turn my head. I didn't know how to respond to it. Derrick didn't, either. We were just way too young to comprehend all this stuff! Relationships are so technical!

We Had to Grow Up

Over the years, we never quite got over our feelings that we had as young kids for one another. We always smiled at one another. We always blushed at one another, and we always flirted when we got a chance.

Then that day finally came. I remember at the end of my 10th grade year, Derrick just happened to be in my neighborhood. It was a beautiful summer day. School was out. We were all just trying to figure out how we were going to spend our summer. Then he came over. He stopped by my house with a friend that day. It was totally unexpected. I came to the door, and when I opened it, my mouth dropped! What in the world was Derrick doing at my house? Well first off, my parents weren't home. I could get in major trouble for this because my brothers would certainly rat me out! So, the first thing I asked him when I opened the door was what in the world was he doing at my house! Now I know that's not a great way of greeting someone. I was shocked, excited and nervous. Yeah, all of that in one!

Derrick smiled at me and told me that he was in my neighborhood and wanted to drop in to see what I was doing. I let him know that he couldn't come in my house because my parents weren't home. I could get in major trouble for that. So I stepped outside and sat on the steps and talked to him. We just kind of did small talk for a minute. Then it came. You know, the relationship talk! Was I ready for that? I don't know, but I did know that I had liked this young man since the first day that I saw him in the 1st grade. That's all I knew. My heart was pounding with excitement. Derrick always knew how to make me feel a certain kind of way.

He jokingly said to me, "I really like you. I want you to be my girlfriend."

I looked at him and said, "Boy, quit playing"! But he wasn't playing. He let me know that he wasn't playing. He was so serious. He saw that I was taking him for a joke and wasn't really serious with him.

Then out of nowhere, this came out of his mouth. "I'll let you cut my hair if you would agree to being my girlfriend". He looked me dead in my face, held my hand, and smiled. I was melting inside.

"Are you for real?" I said to him. He said that he was, and all I needed to do was give him a "yes". I thought, "Man, this would be really cool. I already like him, but cutting his hair would be like me putting my mark on him." You see, being a tomboy, I always tried to do what the guys did. Of course, guys were the ones that cut hair. I thought to myself that it would be really awesome if word got out that I could cut hair, too….and I did it on my new boyfriend! I know this is hilarious, right? But, this is the truth to our story!

That day, I accepted his proposal. I was officially his girlfriend. I said yes. I had given him my hand to starting a new relationship with him. He promised me that he would come back another day and let me cut his hair. Ask me if that day ever came decades of years later!!?? Nope! I can truly say that I got played to give him my "yes"! The brother had a little bit of game!

The Establishment

So, before we get this rolling, I had to get a few things established with my new "boyfriend". He had to know what he was working with!

After school one day, we met at the Jr. Food Mart. It was a small-town convenience store that had a chicken deli in it. It was the place to hang out for all of the high schoolers. Hey, we lived in a small town. What can we say?

Derrick and I met up that day because I had to get some things straight with him. I had just given him my "yes," and I wanted to make sure that we were on the same page when it came to our newfound relationship.

This is what I told him:

"Derrick, I'm so happy that we are now dating! I just want to make sure that we are on the same page. You see, I'm not your typical "around the way girl". When I get in a relationship, I'm serious about the one that I date. Also, I'm not like these other girls who run around and have sex with guys just because. So if you're in this because you think I'm going to have sex with you, then you might want to find you another girlfriend. I am seriously not about games. I'm not about being played. I'm not about wasting my time with a guy who doesn't know what he wants. If you want to date me, then it has to be all about me. No other girl can get in on this. If this is not something you think you can handle, then please let me know up front."

There was a pause. Derrick looked at me and smiled. "Okay", he said. He was ready to go all in. We had gotten our relationship established from the top. We were both now all in. "Let the relationship now officially begin!" I thought.

Don't waste your time, ladies. Be intentional about your dating. Let them know what your ultimate goal is. If they're not with it...move on. That is all.

The Transition

We were in it to win it! We were the best of friends! Dates included hanging out and shooting ball with the guys, laughing and joking, and every now and then, going out to a party. We loved each other so much as teenagers. We really couldn't see being apart from one another.

Then that day came. What happens after high school? What were we going to do? Well, I already knew what I was going to do. Once I set my mind on something, you already know it's DONE!

My mind was made up. I was going to school, and not just any school—Troy State University (now Troy University). I had turned down scholarships. I didn't want to play ball anymore. I solely wanted to focus on my studies. After all, there was no WNBA back then, and I most certainly didn't want to try and play overseas in somebody else's country! Not happening, Captain! So, for me, the decision was easy. I was going to college! I had already taken my ACTs and had done well. I had put in my application and had gotten accepted. I was ready to go! The question now was…what was going to happen with me and Derrick???

I knew that it was time for us to have "the discussion". We had to talk about what our future looked like as individuals and as a couple. I let Derrick know my plans. I was absolutely going to college. There were no other options for me. I had a plan, and I was going to stick to that plan. Derrick, on the other hand, didn't know what he wanted to do. He had this thought about the military because he wasn't sure how college would work for him. He really wanted to go to college and play football (he was a SUPERSTAR on the field). He just didn't have anyone who would push him, who would see to him getting a scholarship. So, in essence, that idea fell to the wayside because the football scholarship plan never happened for him. He lost hope in the idea of him being able to go to college. He was unsure about his next steps, and the only logical idea that made sense to him was the military. I listened to his thoughts carefully. I understood what he was saying. I got it, but I also got something else. This would be the end of our relationship. I knew that if he went into the military and I went to college…our relationship wouldn't make it. I told Derrick that I supported his plan to go into military. I felt his heart. I knew where he was coming from, but I also stated to him clearly that our relationship wouldn't make it. We were entirely too young to have a long-distance relationship like that. He would be off traveling the world with girls galore around him, and I would be thousands of miles away….out of sight, out of mind. I would be on a college campus with guys all around, more than likely trying to talk to me, while Derrick was thousands of miles away…out of sight and out of mind.

We were too young for that type of pressure. I knew that. Though we loved each other dearly, I wasn't sure if we were ready to be tested like that. There was so much of life that we hadn't experienced. I knew that our time had come to move on. I knew that I wanted Derrick to be free when he went off across the world without worrying about what I would say about the people he hung out with or the things that he would perhaps do. I'll be honest. I was afraid of the lying and cheating happening to me, just like it did with my mom and many other women that I saw growing up. I was afraid of the rejection and the hurt that would come from it. What if he cheated with someone and caught a disease and gave it to me? What if I surprised him with a visit and found him with another girl? Listen, those were thoughts that roamed through my head at that very moment. Would Derrick be strong enough to handle the temptation from afar? I'll be honest. I wasn't sure he could. Me on the other hand…I knew I could. I'm not just saying that, either. Remember, when I am committed to someone, I'm committed. I dated with purpose and intention to marry that person. I didn't have eyes for someone else once I committed. I was all in. I knew that I was having fears about Derrick because I was simply afraid of getting hurt. I would stay faithful to him long-distance, but I was afraid that he wouldn't be able to do the same thing. The best thing for me to do was to break it off with him so that we could both move on in peace, not having to worry about what the other was doing thousands of miles away.

I was honest with Derrick. I let him know exactly what I was thinking. I wanted him to understand my heart. I was afraid of losing him to someone else. I wanted to move on with the peace of knowing that I wouldn't have to worry about that when he left for the military. Derrick quietly listened to everything that I said. When I finished talking, his eyes were sad. I knew he didn't like what I had said. Not one bit. He told me that he didn't like it, but he also let me know that he understood where I was coming from. We had a moment of embracing and loving on each other, letting each other know how much our relationship meant to us. It was a beautiful yet sad time. What was I going to do? I felt like he was the love of my life. Was I wrong? We were only kids anyway. What did I know?

Your heart knows the truth. Listen to it. Deep down within, you'll always find the answer.

His Decision was Made

The next day, I was in for a major surprise. Derrick told me that we needed to talk about something. It was serious. He had made a decision. I must admit, I wasn't really sure what was about to come out of his mouth, but I was bracing myself for it. Could it be something that could hurt my feelings? I know what our last discussion had been about. We were going to part ways as we ventured on to the next phase of our lives. Did he want to do it sooner rather than later?

I sat. I listened. I was amazed at what I heard. Total shock and awe moment! Derrick held my hands and looked me in my eyes. He said, "Listen, I don't want to be without you. You are my everything. You mean so much to me. I don't want the military more than I want you. I'm unsure about a lot of things, but one thing that I am most certain of is the idea of me and you being together. So, I have made a decision. I'm not interested in the military anymore. Shoot, I don't think it was ever for me. It was an idea because I didn't know what else to do. I want to pursue the idea of college with you. It excites me. But I don't want to go to any college. I want to go to where you're going, Troy State University. I need your help, though. I don't know anything about the process. Will you help me?"

Did he just say what I think he said? Wait…I'm dreaming right? Well, just pinch me and say it's not a dream then! OMG! He wants to be with me more than he wants the military! Not only are we going to be high school sweethearts, but college sweethearts, too??!! I was in tears. Is this really going to happen? At that moment, my love for Derrick went to a whole new level! He was already willing to sacrifice for ME! We were so young. He was already making sacrifices for me, for us. This was definitely a good sign that he was the one for me!

I expressed my happiness, joy, and gratitude. I was speechless, but at the same time found the words to let him know that I would do everything in my power to make it happen for him! It was on! I was ready. Remember, if I set my mind on something, you can already consider that thing DONE! The same process that I went through, I was willing to do it all over again for him—from application, to ACT test-taking, to doing the prequalification, to filling out his paperwork for Pell grants, seeing if he needed a loan, etc. Oh, it was going to happen if I had anything to do with it. He didn't have to tell me but ONE time!

Needless to say, yes, I got Derrick everything that he needed for school. Yes, I helped get him into TSU. Yes, we went off to college together and endured throughout it all. We were young and in love. College life did bring us some challenges. We probably broke up and got right back together at least 20 times, but we knew that neither one of us were going anywhere. We were meant to be together. Yes, we had the challenge of other guys and girls trying to get in on what we had, but we remained resilient. No matter how hard they tried, no other guy was going to take the place of my guy. I meant that! I wasn't having it! We got through it all and are still shining today.

Derrick majored in psychology and had gotten a minor in human services. I double-majored in Spanish and English. I ended up having to do 2 internships, and it put me graduating a semester behind him. I actually was supposed to graduate in five years instead of four because of the double major, but I refused to let that happen. Nope, not me. If my fiancé was graduating in four years, then this girl right here was going to do the same thing! My mind was made up. So, I went to school every single semester with NO summers off, completing anywhere from 18-21 hours of coursework. It truly was a load for me, and by my last semesters of internships, I was completely burned out. I was tired and wanted to quit; however, I couldn't do it. I was determined to complete the work that I had started!

Derrick and I were planning to have our wedding in August, a few months after my graduation. He had graduated the semester before and had already started working. I'll never forget. We weren't living together before marriage. He had his apartment, and I had mine. I had always worked 2 jobs in college on top of taking a heavy load of classes. But this last semester, I was so burned out from everything, I simply couldn't work. I went to Derrick and asked him if he would allow me to stop working, pay all of my bills (and his bills, too, being that we were living in separate places because we weren't married yet) and allow me to focus solely on my internship, which was pulling on me so much! Derrick agreed to do it with ease! "Like, yeah! I got you! I'll take care of you. Do what you got to do to finish." That's what he told me, and he did just that. He was officially paying for all of my bills before we even got married. Gosh, I love this man!

The Marriage Begins

We were married in August of 2000. We had dated six years before we married. We were engaged five years of the six. We knew we wanted to finish high school and college before we went to the next level in our relationship, which was marriage. We were both very excited to start our lives as not just a couple anymore, but a married couple.

We moved to Panama City, Florida. Foreign land. Different. No family. No friends. Just us. This whole thing was new to us, but we were willing to embark on this journey together.

Even though we had dated for all of those years, being married was totally new. We began to know each other at a more intimate and deeper level than ever before. Remember, my husband and I never "shacked up" before marriage. This was our first time actually living together as a couple. Totally new to both of us!

When we had gotten to Panama City, we were excited. But frustration soon sat in. We realized that we had gotten bamboozled. We had gotten tricked. I was recruited down there on a two for one deal. If I came, they would hire my husband as well and give him a job in the school system as a counselor. Okay, let me back up. I was recruited to go to Panama City to teach Spanish at Rutherford High School. Our recruiter that came to TSU promised me that if I signed with them, they would also bring on my husband since he had gotten his degree in psychology. Long story short (you have to read my book *Faith in a Barren Land* to hear the whole story. It will blow your mind!), we were lied to. I got the job, but they completely forgot to give my husband "his job". It put us in a very challenging situation financially. Wait…we had just gotten married. We were still newlyweds. Did we have to deal with financial instability at the beginning of our marriage?? The answer to that was yes. Our marriage struggled early on in the area of finances; however, my husband and I made up in our minds that we were not going to let that affect what we meant to one another. I didn't marry him for money, and money sure wasn't going to be the downfall of what we had waited all these years to do!

Instead of there being friction in our marriage, there was encouragement. I remember encouraging my husband constantly on who he is. I remember saying things like, *"We're going to get through this. The turnaround is here. God is going to bless us. We're going to have more than enough soon."* I refused to let finances tear our marriage apart. For a man, it's hard when you feel like you can't take care of your family. I knew it was hard for my husband. I knew the enemy would play tricks with his mind. I knew this was a test for us, but I also knew that we would pass with flying colors!

And we did just that. Nothing was going to stop us. To this day, my husband thanks me for encouraging him and giving him strength during one of the hardest times of our marriage.

Ladies, when you see your husband in a low place in any area, it's your job to build him up, not tear him down.

This was my first big moment of dealing with him. I had to deal with the insecurities that evolved from our financial situation. I had to deal with those moments of lowliness. I had to figure out a way to get him out of the pit so that he could lead our home financially. What I love about my husband is that he will do what is necessary. He will make it happen! He loves to make me happy, and he was willing to do what it took to do just that. So, he began working three jobs to make ends meet. He worked hard. He was diligent, steadfast and determined for us to win in the area of finances. Then one day...it happened. God opened a door for one job to provide more money than the three jobs ever could! You really have to read *Faith in a Barren Land*. I can't go into all of the details here, but I will say this...my husband is THE MAN! I love him. To stand by him during one of the hardest times we had at the very onset of our marriage was an honor and a privilege for me.

I began to wonder...why did we have a financial test at the very beginning of our marriage? Like seriously, we hadn't been married but a few months, and this happened! Maybe God was testing us to see if we could endure the financial storm. Maybe He wanted to see what foundation our marriage was based on. We all know that finances is one of the top reasons why marriages fail. But I promise you, it will never be a reason why our marriage fails. We will be broke together, blue-collar workers together, rich together, or millionaires together. We will have our pork and beans and weenies together, and we will have our steak and potatoes together. It doesn't matter. Money may rule the world, but it will NOT rule our marriage!

Money matters. Don't get me wrong. I know this. With money, you can do a lot of things. Without it, you can struggle through a lot of things, but in the end, it's up to you and your spouse how you handle it. I'm going to go into more money talk in the money chapter, but I wanted you to know how I had to deal with him when it came to our finances. He was and is first. He was and is everything to me that money can't be. We will struggle together, and we will win together. Money won't ever change that for our marriage. I challenge you to not let it change yours.

Dealing with Him. Dealing with Me. Make the Decision.

We were in this for the long haul. We both knew that. We also knew we had to figure out how to deal with each other—flaws and all. Love conquers a multitude of things. It was about to start conquering because we realized sooner rather than later that we both had issues.

Then it began. Marriage is actually pretty different than dating. In a marriage, you discover your spouse at a whole new level. It's not the dating game anymore. It's the marriage life. It rocks, but it's work all at the same time.

So here we are, trying to figure out life together as a married couple. I soon realized that one of the things that I had to deal with was leading. Okay, let me make it plain. My husband had NO clue what it took to lead our home or our marriage. Now listen…this is not a put-down for him. This is something that we often talk about with other couples in order to help them overcome the same issues that we had. So again, he had no clue how to lead.

Making a decision for our house/marriage was a challenge oftentimes for my husband. It would be something as simple as establishing where we were going out for dinner, or what is it that he would like to do, where we were going to be in the next few years, etc. His answer the majority of the time would be, "I don't know. What do you think?"

Ladies, I must say, this IRKED me soooo bad! OMG…can you just please make a decision? Lead me. Tell me where we are going. Tell me what we are doing. Tell me what you want. His being unsure about everything stirred up frustration inside of me. You see, that's where my husband and I were different. I always knew what I wanted, and I went after it. My husband, on the other hand, was always unsure of what he wanted and was indecisive. It spilled over into how he led our house. We were young. We were both trying to figure this thing out. I will admit that at first, I didn't handle it well. I was so frustrated with him and would ask him why he wasn't sure about anything. Why was it that he always went back and forth with decisions? It showed me instability in his leading, so I became extremely frustrated. I would tell him that I needed him to be more secure. It would often bring arguments and frustration on both ends.

He didn't know how to be the man. I didn't know how to show the support to help him be the man. We were about to figure this thing out, though.

You see, my husband didn't have the example that he needed growing up. His dad was laid-back, indecisive, go with the flow, not really secure, not really adamant. He was only exemplifying what he saw growing up. When it was time for him to step into the same position, he repeated what was shown to him growing up as a child. I'll just say this…being the type of woman that I am, that wasn't going to work for me. I always had direction. If I didn't have it, I would find it. I knew what I wanted. I always had a plan, and I always backed that plan up with action, so this was new to me. I didn't experience this with my husband when we were dating. Shoot, we were just having fun. Leading wasn't necessary. But now…things had changed. You got to get with it, Sir! We got stuff to do and places to go!

I didn't know how to help him. My way of helping him was showing my frustration about him not knowing how to lead. I saw that the frustration was not helping him get better. It made him shy away even more from leading. I had to change the way that I approached him. Now that I think about it, I think my frustration may have come across as more disrespectful than anything. No, I didn't curse him out or call him names. I just questioned him on why he couldn't make a decision. A lot. Yeah, I did it a lot because he was faced with this challenge a lot. So, I became less aggressive in my approach. I learned how to suggest things to him to see if he could decide rather than demand a decision from him. I learned how to encourage him in his decision making. I wanted and needed him to feel like the man that could lead our home well. We had to get this thing right before the kids came! We had to get it all the way together!

I also knew that being around other men with dynamic leadership would help him. There was only so much that I would be able to do. So, we got connected to a church that we later joined. It was perfect for that time and season in our life. My husband was able to connect with these men. He was built up even more through the Pastor and the other leaders in that church. I can honestly say that it helped our marriage tremendously! My husband was finally around someone who could help him understand his role as the head of our home. I thank God for that!

Ladies, one of the biggest mistakes that we can make is to frustrate our men when they want to do better, but have no clue as to how to get to that "better". People don't know things that they've never been taught. They walk in ignorance to it. Ignorance can sometimes bring frustration to those around them. Why? Because the expectation is that you already know something, and because you are supposed to already know something, the only thing to do now is to do what you supposedly already know. When you don't do what you're "supposed to know", disappointment comes to those who were expecting you to. There are things that frustrated me so much about my husband, but getting frustrated with him about things that he honestly had no clue how to do only brought in confusion in our home. I had to find a better way to help my husband get better. In helping him get better, WE got better. I had to learn how to hush. I had to learn how to encourage. I had to learn how to be patient as he grew in understanding in how to take the lead in our marriage. I had to learn how to walk beside him in support in every phase of his "learning". Sometimes it was a challenge, but in the end, I can honestly say it's been worth it. My husband does an amazing job in leading our family now. He's not perfect, but he is amazing. I love that man!

There are other things that I had to learn how to deal with as well. These things include how my husband communicated. Oh, communication is such a big thing! Whew! It can make or break a relationship for sure! Instead of talking about that in this chapter, I will wait until the communication chapter to really dive in.

In a nutshell, once my husband and I learned how to deal better with one another, our marriage went to another level. As a matter of fact, it continues to go to another level after decades of being married. Oftentimes, we look at each other and talk about how amazing it is to still have "it" after all these years. He still makes me blush. I make him feel like "the man". He still gets me flowers. We still send each other love notes. We're still dating like teenagers. We're still constantly loving and growing with each other every single day. That's one of the things that make our marriage fabulous. We never stop trying. We purpose to grow beyond measure every single day of our lives. I challenge you to do the same. In dealing with him and him dealing with you, you learn how to deal the right way in your marriage if you do it the right way. Things will only keep getting better through thick and through thin. The key is you both have to want it. You both have to learn. You both have to love, respect, and honor each other, no matter the circumstance, trial or tribulation. Sometimes that's easier said than done, but remember, it's doable. If we can do it, then so can you. Deal with it…the right way. You'll thank me for it later.

Chapter 5

The Scoreboard.
Who's Winning?

The Scoreboard. Who's Winning?

Imagine this. It's the championship game. The game of your life, perhaps the most important game that you will ever play. You're in the last quarter of the game. The score keeps going back and forth. You're up. They're up. You're down. They're winning. You fight harder, and now you're up. Time is winding down. It's a tie game with seconds left on the clock. You feel like you're the MVP of the team, so you want the ball. As a matter of fact, you're demanding the ball. The attention should be on you as you ARE the best player on the team. You ARE the point guard, right? You already know how to score. You know how to win. You've been doing it all your life. This was the game of all games, and you are determined to outscore your opponent. You're determined to win. Seconds are left on the clock. The ball is in your hands. Your teammate is wide open on the right side. Instead of passing him the ball, you feel like you're the all-star, and you should take the final shot, the final blow. It's all on you. As you dribble towards the basket, ignoring your teammate, you throw the ball up. It's going...going...going. It looks like it's going to go in, but it abruptly hits the backboard so hard. It's a brick. Seconds go off the clock. The game is over. Your team loses. Your teammate looks at you and wonders why you were so selfish to take that shot. You were NOT open. You should have trusted your team to help you out, but instead you doubted and took the game into your own hands and did what you wanted to do, which in turn cost you the game of your life. It was over. There was nothing you could do at this point but go back and apologize to your team for taking such a DUMB shot. Instead, pride won't let you be great. You keep your mouth closed. Head is in the air. You tell everyone "good game" and walk away to be by yourself. You don't realize the power of being humble in that moment. Instead, you replay in your head how you could have changed your shot up just a little bit so that you could make the basket. You never once considered your teammate in this. Pride won't let you or your team be GREAT. Instead, it causes you to be a loser.

Isn't that how it often goes in marriages? Your marriage is the game of your life. If you play it well, it ends well. If you play badly, it goes badly. If you become selfish, your teammate gets mad at you, but because you're so determined to "win", you're so determined to "get your point across", you're so determined to be the "best player on the team", you never really consider how they feel or what they feel. You just need to get your point across because you're going to "show them" who the real MVP is. Nobody is getting over on you, right?

Here's another situation. Have you ever found yourself keeping score of what they did to you in the game? The number of times they turned the ball over? The number of times they missed a shot? The number of times they missed a layup? The number of times they threw up a brick? Or let me put it this way…how about the number of times they got an attitude, mistreated you, lied, cheated, disrespected you, didn't do something you asked them to do or said something crazy to you? The list can go on and on. Are you one that finds yourself keeping a scorecard of the number of times these things happened? How's that going for you? Who's winning? You or him? Who has the most points? Is the moral of the game that whoever has the most points wins? Or do they lose? Only you know. But I can tell you this…your spouse is not your opponent. As I recall, you're actually on the SAME team. So why is it that sometimes we act as if we're trying to "win" against the other.

After decades of being married, I can honestly say that my husband and I found ourselves doing this early on in our marriage. We were young! What else can I say? It took some time for us to figure out that we were actually on the same team.

You see, you don't need a scorecard to remind your spouse of the number of times they did you dirty. You don't need to throw it up in their face every time you get mad. You don't need to belittle them in order to feel like you're winning.

Early on in our marriage, I can say that I was the MVP of that. Oh, I can tell you the day, the time, the month, and the year! There's a whole list. You want to see it? I can tell my husband, "You know that one time when I asked you to do this, and you didn't do it…or that one time, when you said this to me…or that one time when you did that to me? You're still doing it. You haven't gotten better. You're the same or worse." Yeah, we ladies can give a breakdown like no other! Or is it just me?? Hmm…well, I'm being transparent right now, and if that's you or used to be you, then I'm sure you can relate. Oh, and don't let it be anything that really hurt you like lying or cheating. You try so hard to forgive and stick with it, but you constantly remind him of the dirt he did to you. You let him know that he'll never change. Instead of encouraging him, you discourage him! You know why? Because you never really forgave. You're still going through the motions of trying to figure out how to forgive. But instead, you place him in the position of being your opponent, and you keep a score sheet of all the wrongs he did. Will you ever get healed? Will you ever let go? Or do you like holding all of that bitterness inside and constantly reminding him of how evil he is? How's that going for you? It can't be going that well. If anything, your marriage will get worse and not better. You will remain bitter over past circumstances and situations that you swear you're over, but for some odd reason, they keep coming up! What's that all about?

When you choose to let go, you have to really let go. You can't keep this record in your head and play it every time you get mad. You have to learn to be free. You have to learn to break free. You have to let go of the old and embrace the new. If anything, you discourage the man from becoming better. He would rather be on the roof of a house than stay inside while you rehash all of the horrible things of his past, or the ways that he's not being a good husband or the number of times that he missed the mark. In a man's eyes, that's a form of disrespect. I know it sounds weird when you feel like they're wrong, but I promise you, if you keep coming in a man's face with issues and accusations, the way you come across to him can often appear to be disrespectful. Instead of being around that, he wants to flee. He'll let you win. He's tired of hearing it. Call him whatever you want to call him. He's out. Eventually, if it doesn't get figured out soon, divorce is inevitable because the communication between the two of you is horrible. Nobody sees their part. Each person sees the wrong in the other. Coming up with a better way to express those wrongs is key, but instead, we keep scores and remind each other of who's winning.

Ladies, I have come to tell you right now. That will NEVER work. Whatever it is that you have issues with, you've got to figure out a way to be free. You have to forgive. You have to let go. You have to trust God. You have to know that nagging, fussing, cussing, and belittling isn't working. However you choose to get your point across, you have to be real with yourself. Is it working or not? Evaluate. Assess. Make necessary changes. Your husband is not your opponent. He's actually the captain of your team who needs respect and honor in order to lead the team well. Is he perfect? Nope. But if you chose to love and forgive him, then your job is to assist him in winning championships for your marriage instead of losing it all.

Here are a few questions to ask yourself when you begin thinking that your marriage is a competition.

1. Is my spouse my partner or my enemy? Too many times in our marriage, we begin to view our mate as the enemy. He is not the enemy! *"For our struggle is not against flesh and blood, but against the rulers, against the powers, against the world forces of this darkness, against the spiritual forces of wickedness in the heavenly places" (Ephesians 6:12 NASB).* Don't treat him as the enemy, but rather as your partner or teammate.

2. Am I working toward oneness? A covenant marriage is meant to reflect Christ's relationship with the Church. The Church cannot function properly without Christ as the head of the Church. The Church will not function properly without each member doing their part within the body of Christ. The same is true for the marriage relationship. Each spouse has to do his/her part in order for the marriage to function properly. We have to function as one.

3. Am I focusing on Me or We? I believe that Ephesians 5:21, which says, *"and be subject to one another in the fear of Christ,"* carries over into the following discussion of marriage in verses 22-33. Therefore, the role of each spouse is one of submission to each other as you would submit to Christ. If we focus on ME, we lose sight of Christ. If we focus on our spouse, we lose sight of Christ. We need to focus on WE, which includes Christ. This shift in our focus will bring about the intimacy that is truly desired.

Don't Keep Score. Your marriage is not a competition. It is a journey toward intimacy that God planned from the very beginning. Are you working toward that goal? Think about it and answer honestly. Whatever changes you need to make, make them. Reaching the next level in your marriage depends upon it.

Chapter 6

Submit, Respect, Obey—
Say What!?

Submit, Respect, Obey—Say What!?

- **Submit**- to give or yield to the power or authority of another.
- **Respect**- esteem for or a sense of worth or excellence of a person, a personal quality or ability, or something considered as a manifestation of a personal quality or ability; to hold in esteem or honor.
- **Obey**- to comply with or follow the commands, restrictions, wishes, or instructions of; to submit or conform in action to (some guiding principle, impulse, one's conscience, etc.).

That's a lot to take in. I really believe I need to break down each one of those individually and then address them as a whole, so let's get started.

SUBMISSION

For many women, this word is a curse word! Yep. It's like you're cursing us. What do you mean submission?? What does that look like? Does that mean we get treated like little puppy dogs hoping and wishing that our Master would play with us, give us treats and be our best friend? What does submission actually look like?

Growing up, as stated earlier, I didn't see a lot of healthy, beautiful, and prosperous marriages around me. My mom and dad loved each other, but their marriage wasn't great. I remember seeing my mom "submit" to my dad. She would get up super early to cook his breakfast and make his lunch. She would make sure dinner was ready for him. She would oftentimes do whatever he wanted. In the process of that, I witnessed my mom being abused, lied to and cheated on. When she tried to fight back, she would never win. She was the "weaker vessel", and because she was weaker, it was hard for her to win over my dad. For years, I saw physical abuse and emotional abuse. I often questioned why my mom would submit to that. Why would she be "okay" with someone doing all of the things that my dad used to do to her? I could never understand during that time of my life. I'm happy to say that my dad one day had a complete change of heart. He vowed to never lay hands on my mom again, and he didn't; however, the damage had already been done. I had seen and heard too much. My brothers had seen and heard too much. We were scarred. We had some things that we had to fight through and deal with growing up. It wasn't easy because all we genuinely wanted was to have a happy home like everyone else. Don't get me wrong. Every day wasn't chaotic. We had some great times, but isn't it funny how those really bad days always stand out more than the good days? You have more good days than bad, but you can always remember the intricate parts of those bad days. It can leave you with emotions that can scar you for the rest of your days if you don't choose to deal with it, get over it and forgive whomever needs forgiving.

In a nutshell, I thought submission was of the devil. I saw my mom submit and get treated like dirt. I saw her being controlled and manipulated. What I saw the most was that I wanted NO parts in all of that stuff! No man was going to control me. No man was going to manipulate me, beat on me, or emotionally abuse me....no man! I would not be like my mom. That's what I said when it came to being a wife and submitting. I saw her do it, and I saw where it got her. I didn't want to ever go through that! Ever!

Of course, that led to relationship issues for me. I had to be hard-core. I had to let him know that I don't care who you are, no man was going to get over on me. I'm not weak. I'm strong. I can do what I want. I can have what I desire! My desire was to have a husband that loved me, honored me and treated me like a queen! I wasn't going to submit to foolishness. Nope. Not this one.

I didn't know that my hurt and pain from my childhood was actually bringing hurt and pain into my relationship with my husband. I thought that if I submitted to my husband, I would look weak, that he would think he could do and say anything to me and it would be okay. I thought that submission would never work for me. It had never worked in past relationships, so why would it work for me right now?

In submitting to my husband, it showed honor and respect to him. The one thing that men desire the most is respect. You show a man respect, and you've got him. When a man feels disrespected, look out world. There have been many a fights and battles all because of that one word—disrespect.

I've learned that it's easy for a man to love a wife who honors, submits, and respects him. It's easy for a wife to love a man who treats her like a queen. When a man gets treated like a king, there's nothing he wouldn't do for that woman. It's all about respect for them and love for the wife.

So why is it so hard to submit? What's the problem here?

The Bible tells us in Ephesians 5:22 to *"Submit yourselves unto your own husbands as unto the Lord."* It then says again in Colossians 3:18, *"Wives, submit yourselves unto your own husbands, as it is fitting in the Lord."* So, I ask you now, if we can't submit to our husbands, how can we submit to God? The world will tell us that submission is not necessary, that obeying our husbands or following their lead leaves us weak and dependent. I even thought that myself. I learned that my non-submission, hardness, and ruggedness was causing more problems in my marriage than solutions. But the Bible says, *"And be not conformed to this world: but be ye transformed by the renewing of your mind, that ye may prove what is that good, and acceptable, and perfect, will of God" (Romans 12:2).* And what is the will of God? That we submit ourselves to our husbands. The world may not understand submission, but we are not to be conformed to this world.

Submission and obedience go hand in hand. Wives, we must submit and obey our husbands, but there is a balance to all of that. It sounds so challenging, but ladies, I promise you it's doable. I was reading an article from a man who gave reasons why his wife should obey him. I thought it was an interesting topic, so of course, I had to see what he was talking about it. Let me share it with you, and we'll discuss this afterwards.

Five Reasons Why My Wife Should Obey Me by Scott Morefield
1) I love her

The Bible says we should love Christ BECAUSE Christ first loved us. Paul also compares male headship of the house to Christ being the head of the church. Loving our wives is God's primary command to us toward them (Ephesians 5:25). If we love our wives as we are called to do, to the point of chivalry, consideration, protection, and self-sacrifice, it's naturally easy for the wife to submit to her husband. After all, she knows he has her best interest at heart.

2) I consider her my equal

In the eyes of God, there is no Jew or Greek, no male or female (Galatians 3:28). This doesn't mean there aren't hierarchies of "command" here on earth, but is a 5-star general any more loved by God than a 4-star general, or even a private (yeah kids, that's you – better keep practicing those salutes and "yes, sirs" and "ma'ams!" :))? Of course not! There is nothing "demeaning" to the wife because she is Biblically submissive to her husband.

3) In leadership, two is a crowd

In every successful organization, from churches to businesses to schools to armies to nations, while responsibilities are shared, ultimately the buck stops somewhere, and that somewhere is the person at the top. The truth is, life is full of hierarchies, and they aren't all bad.

An organization with more than one CEO, like a ship with more than one rudder, ultimately goes nowhere. Imagine if there were two Presidents with equal powers. Although both understand and agree that football is the best sport (duh!), one wants to invade Canada and stop hockey (because we all know hockey really should be stopped!) while the other wants to invade South America to rid the hemisphere of soccer. All are admirable goals, but do we really have the capacity to conduct both operations efficiently? I think not.

While the person in charge should certainly get advice from those he is responsible for, someone has to make the final decision. Common sense says, otherwise, nothing of consequence gets done.

4) I seek her input

A husband would be foolish to never seek the counsel of his wife (OK maybe Job should have left it alone, but that's a topic for another day!). What kind of leader never asks for the advice of his co-workers? A horribly ineffective one! While the husband should be the head of his home, marriage is ultimately a partnership. Two heads are always better than one. Obtaining my wife's counsel and seeking her consent, especially on decisions of consequence, is an important part of a thriving relationship. God gave us our wives to be our helpmates, the other halves of our whole. Their unique point of view is meant to balance, and often temper ours.

Ultimately, the principle of "headship" is important. The man, as the "head", has a duty to listen to all the other parts of the body. He is responsible to his family and finally to God for the decisions he makes. A wise husband will always heavily consider the counsel of his wife. In our marriage, my wife and I will sometimes disagree strongly on something. We'll hash it out, and usually, eventually, we come to a compromise or even total agreement. Rarely is there ever a fork in the road where I make a decision that she disagrees with, but she respects my position as head of our household to make those decisions when they must be made. For me, that is a heavy responsibility never to be taken lightly. I always ask for her advice, and it is with great prayer and trepidation that I EVER make a decision without the consent of my wife.

5) The Bible says so

I realize this isn't going to fly with non-Christians, but to Christians who are reading this – as much as I hate to play this card, I'm gonna... I didn't write it, God did! In the most fundamental building block of society, the family, God happens to have ordained the man to be the head of the house. In order for the holy state of matrimony to accurately reflect the nature of Christ's relationship with His church, it has to be this way.

Okay, a few caveats
– because, as you could imagine, this is a principle that has been heavily abused in history and even by some Christians today:

1) It is NEVER a man's responsibility to "make" his wife obey him.

That is always her choice, and ultimately is between her and God. To the man who has an unbelieving or un-submissive spouse, my advice would be to work on the principles and directives given to the husband – namely self-sacrificing love, chivalry, and affection; pray for her, and let God work in her heart. In the end, the only person we can change is ourselves, so (obviously) don't be a bully!

2) True Biblical submission is always a give and take.

The Bible, while ordaining male headship of the household, also commands both parties to render benevolence to each other (I Corinthians 7:3). And again, it commands the husband to love his wife, to give himself for her as Christ gave Himself for the church.

3) Utilize, don't suppress, the talents and capacities God has given your wife.

The Proverbs 31 woman considered a field and bought it. Be a good delegator! And just as she should for you, support your wife in her interests and endeavors, especially as she uses her unique talents for the Lord.

So there you have it, the principle of Biblical submission from a traditional Christian male point of view. While I fully understand that this isn't a popular stand nowadays, I truly hope those of you whose knees are (understandably) jerking back into your chest will prayerfully consider this view in light of Scripture and common sense.

When the wife fulfills her God-given purpose and role in the home, she truly exemplifies the poetic words of Solomon, "The heart of her husband doth safely trust in her, so that he shall have no need of spoil. She will do him good and not evil all the days of her life." Proverbs 31: 11-12

Okay. So I can say that I agree with Scott. He made some very valid points based on the Word of God as to why his wife should submit to him. He loves her. He considers her his equal. There can be only one head. He seeks her input, and most importantly, the Bible says so! I absolutely concur with everything; however, there are some women who get it, but based on "their situation", they still have a hard time doing it.

Let's explore a couple of reasons why women have a super hard time in submitting to their husbands.

Shocking News

A majority of wives want to submit to their husbands. They want their husbands to be the head of the home, and they have no desire to usurp that God-given position of leadership. They know what the Bible says on the subject. Discerning wives want to do what God wants because they understand that God's ways work best. However, problems often arise in this area because a wife is afraid to submit to her husband for two reasons:

Reason #1:

Her husband thinks submission is only a noun, and he uses it as a weapon.

Reason #2:

Her husband has himself not made the choice in his heart to be fully submitted to God.

Okay, okay! I know that God did not say a wife needs to submit to her husband only if he proves to be worthy. Submission is a matter of trusting in God more than trusting in man, but a wife will more easily make the choice to submit to her husband if she knows that he has made the choice to submit to the Lord. It will be a sign to her that it is safe to submit to him. And the goal here is to help her, not force her into proper alignment.

Trusting

Some women have a hard time trusting that their husband is hearing from God if he doesn't appear to be submitted to God in the way that he treats her. Wives know that after the verse *"Wives, submit to your own husbands,"* (Ephesians 5:22), the Bible says, *"Husbands, love your wives, just as Christ also loved the church and gave Himself for her"* (verse 25).

Christ doesn't neglect, ignore, demean, or abuse the Church. He doesn't treat her rudely or disrespectfully. He never acts arrogantly or insensitively towards her, nor does He criticize her and make her feel that she is not valuable. Rather He loves her, protects her, provides for her, and cares for her. So, while God gives the husband a position of leadership in relationship to his wife, He also requires the price of self-sacrifice from him.

When Wives Hold Back

The big question in many women's minds is, "If I submit myself to my husband, will I become a doormat for him to walk on?" The answer to that question depends entirely upon whether her husband believes he should love his wife like Christ loves the Church. Does he willingly sacrifice himself for her or think that submission is a noun and that it is something owed to him? In other words, does he only consider his desires and opinions, to the exclusion of hers?

A wife has a hard time giving her husband the reins to her life if she doesn't believe she can trust him to have her best interests at heart as he steers the course of their lives together. She has trouble going along with his decisions when he refuses to consider her thoughts, feelings, and insights on the subject. And if she has submitted to a male in the past and her trust was violated in some way, it is even more difficult for her to trust now.

On the Other Hand

A woman will do anything for a man who loves her like Christ loves the Church. Submission is easy under these conditions. I know a number of women who are married to unbelieving husbands. They have no problem submitting to their husbands. This is because in each case, the husband loves his wife like Christ loves the Church, even though he doesn't know Christ.

Can't Demand Submission

Submission means "to submit yourself". In light of that, when a husband *demands* submission from his wife, it is no longer true submission. And his demands can become intimidating and oppressive, which breeds resentment. When a husband is more interested in his wife's submission to him than he is in his own submission to God, then submission becomes a tool to hurt and destroy.

I have seen too many marriages between strong Christian people—high-profile Christian leaders, in fact—end in divorce because the husband demanded submission and resorted to verbal or physical abuse in order to get it. My husband has even counseled men like that, men who refused to hear that losing their family was a horrible price to pay for being "right". How much better it would have been for the husband to submit himself to God's hand and then pray for his wife to be able to come into proper order. This kind of situation occurs far too often.

God Frees Us

When we submit to God, He doesn't suppress who we are. He frees us to become who we're made to be, within the boundaries of His protection. When a wife submits to her husband, she comes under his covering and protection, and this frees her to become all that God created her to be. Trust me. Every husband wants that for his wife. Her greatest gifts will prove to be his greatest blessing.

In essence, when we as wives learn to respect our husbands and submit, it makes our marriage easier, especially when the husband is doing his job at loving the wife. I had to take a good look at my marriage and find the areas in which I could do better. This was one of those areas. It took humility to do that. I had to surrender my prideful ways and submit to a man that I know genuinely loves me and will do anything in the world for me. He takes good care of me. He's a great provider for our family. He does whatever I ask of him. He tells me all the time that his job is to outthink me when it comes to needs and desires. He wants to position himself to meet that need without me even asking him. He is amazing, I will admit. I am not perfect in my submission. I do have prideful moments; I like to call them "spoiled brat kind of moments". I have to gather myself and check my emotions and see what's really going on. Through it all, I purpose in my heart daily to do a better job of submitting to the love of my life. He has done so much for me, and I have done so much for him. We submit one to the other. He loves me like Christ loves the Church.

Does he have his moments as well? Oh, absolutely! He has moments where I have to question him about something he said or did, but we both purposed in our hearts to be quick to get it right! We are not going days without talking and setting the record straight like we would do in the past! Oh yeah, back in the day, I could act like he wasn't even in the house with me! Yep, I would walk around for days like I didn't even see him, even though he was there every day! I'd say we had some very childish moments. The beauty of it all is that we have been able to grow together, love together, become better together. We hold each other accountable for our actions and for our words. We understand that if it's going to work, it's going to take teamwork. He has to give 100%, and I do too. It's not a 50/50 type situation with us. It's a we're all in, in it to win it, down with each other like four flat tires type of situation! That's why I can share and write this book with you. After decades of being together, we have had years of trial and error, and years of figuring out what works and what doesn't work. Here's a key to that: when you figure out what doesn't work, it's up to you to stop it and do something different. If you don't, you'll keep doing the same thing but expecting different results. We all know what that's called—INSANITY! Let's not be insane when it comes to our marriages. Let's be humble, submitted, and committed to go to the next level. It will work if you work it. I'm a living witness to it!

Here are a few everyday ways to practice submitting to your husband. I believe these simple strategies will help take your marriage to another level!

♦ **First and foremost...submit yourself to the Lord.** This will be your motivation, your guide, your right perspective and where you will find joy and strength. God is the head over your marriage...over both you and your husband

(Matthew 22:37-38; 1 Chronicles 16:25-27; Exodus 20:1-3).

♦ **Always remember that your husband is your sweetheart and lovingly care for him as you want him to love and care for you.** Yeah, it doesn't matter how mad he makes you, ladies. At the end of the day, it's not worth lingering. Don't waste precious time arguing and being mad over something. Enjoy your sweetheart. Love on him. Don't let pride get in the way of that (Song of Songs 2:3; Matthew 7:12).

♦ **Pray for a greater understanding of what God wants you to do** in your relationship with your husband and in your role in the marriage. The Bible tells us that in all our getting, we need to get some understanding
(Jeremiah 33:3; James 1:5)!

♦ **Recognize that marriage isn't about who is in control; it should always be God** (2 Chronicles 20:6).

♦ **Acknowledge and accept that God has placed your husband in this position of leadership over you as his wife (Ephesians 5:22-24).**

♦ **Acknowledge the Holy Spirit's role in all this.** He has the power to change hearts and direct both of you. Always trust and rely on Him to lead you. **Remember, your submission to your husband is *"as to the Lord"*** (Ephesians 5:22).

♦ **Trust the Lord and His plan and take each step forward in faith**
(Proverbs 3:5-6).

♦ **Respectfully share your opinions and possible solutions with your husband** regarding issues that arise and decisions that must be made. You know, we as women can be very emotional about things dear to us. Don't let your emotions overtake the conversation (Ephesians 5:33).

♦ When decisions must be made and you don't agree, **allow your husband to make the final decision** and trust God for the outcome (Titus 2:4-5).

♦ **Resist the urge to take control of any situation.** That's right. Part of the reason why men feel a certain way as the head is because many wives won't let them lead. They feel the need to "take control". Listen, you don't have to be in control of everything. Trust God. Trust your husband. Let him lead. If he makes a mistake, give him the opportunity to learn from it, grow from it, and become better from it (Luke 9:23; Romans 8:9).

♦ **Pray *for* your husband.** All the time. Yep…all the time ☺ (Ephesians 1:16-19).

♦ **Pray *with* your husband** (Matthew 18:20).

♦ **Allow him to lead in couple/family devotions** (Ephesians 5:22-30). (If this isn't something he already does, pray that the Lord will give him the desire. Talk to him in a loving way about your desire to have these times together.)

♦ **Never undermine your husband's authority by going behind his back** to do something you know he would not like (Ephesians 5:22, 33).

♦ **Put him above all others (except God)**...with your time, your service, and your choices (Ephesians 5:31).

♦ **Consider him in *all* of your personal decisions.** (Remember, you are one.) With bigger decisions, ask your husband's opinion and ask him to pray with you to make the best choice (Matthew 19:4-6; Matthew 18:20).

♦ **Give yourself to your husband physically and enjoy expressing your love for him intimately.** Don't deprive the man of his goodies. For goodness sake, they're his! I can't wait to talk to you more on this in the SEX chapter ☺
(1 Corinthians 7:2-4; Song of Songs 4:16)!

♦ **Listen to him when he wants to talk and don't get upset when he doesn't want to.** If communication is an issue for you guys, pray about it and ask God to help you with it (James 1:19-20; Ephesians 4:2-3).

♦ **Give him grace.** He has a tough job as leader and needs the Lord just as much as you do to fulfill his calling in the marriage (Proverb 22:11; Romans 16:20; Ephesians 5:25-27).

♦ **Humble yourself.** Submission is all about humility. Non-submission is all about pride. The Bible talks about how God gives grace to the humble, but the prideful He brings to a low place. In learning how to submit, you learn how to humble yourself (1 Peter 3:8; Psalm 25:9).

♦ **Deny your own wants and desires when they conflict with his.** Usually this is the other way around, but at times, you may be challenged with this. Accept the challenge. It's not that bad. Be like Nike and just do it. A blessing will come from it (Philippians 2:3-4).

♦ **Respect your husband.** Respect is an inseparable part of submission. Respect the fact that he may sin and fall short and needs the Lord just like you do. Respect his opinion as valid and valuable. Respect his feelings. (He has them, even if he doesn't express them). Respect his role as head over you and your family
(Proverbs 31:23; Ephesians 5:33).

♦ **Take care of the things that he asks you to take care of. This is working together in oneness.** For instance, in our house, I'm in charge of the day-to-day finances. We've talked about how we should handle our money, and I make the daily decisions based on what we've discussed. If there are bigger purchases or changes in our financial plan, I discuss them with my husband before I make them, especially if I'm unsure how best to proceed. We'll talk more on this in the money chapter (Proverbs 31:27).

♦ **Respect his desires even when he isn't able to be a part of something.** Such instances might include an illness, travel away from home, or being unable to contact him. Knowing your husband's way of doing things, his preferences, and what he has led both of you to do in the past will help in making those daily decisions to submit to his authority. **And when you're unsure, pray for the wisdom and strength to make the right choice** (Proverbs 31:11-12; Colossians 3:23-24).

Be careful not to use these situations as a way to take advantage to get your own way. This only separates you and destroys oneness (Leviticus 25:17).

♦ **Don't be resentful. Or get angry. Or sulk. Or tell all your friends all about how foolish you think your husband is.** At the end of the day, they're not sleeping next to him. You are. Y'all will make up and be all right. So, don't leave a tainted impression of your husband in the minds of others. That's your husband! Protect who he is and who he is becoming (Titus 3:1-2)!

♦ **Give your insecurity and fears over to the Lord** (Isaiah 41:10; Psalm 118:6).

♦ **Always keep praying for God to give wisdom and direction to your husband** so he will lead you and your family in God's ways and always make the right decisions for you (Colossians 4:2; Ephesians 1:17).

♦ **"Leave" your father and mother.** They are no longer in authority over you. God has given that place to your husband. When you married and became one with each other, you separated from your childhood families to form your own. Seeking what God wants the two of you to do together should be your main consideration, not what your parents think or desire for you. Still love them and care for them, but you are no longer in submission to them (Genesis 2:24; Ephesians 5:23).

♦ If there is something your husband wants you to do that you believe goes against the Lord and His ways, respectfully and lovingly go to him and show him in God's Word why you believe this, and pray for God to change his mind. But if he refuses to change, you must respectfully

refuse to submit to his sinful desire and choose instead to submit to the Lord. **A biblical wife always submits first to the Lord**
(Acts 4:19-20; Proverbs 31:30; Ephesians 4:14-15).

♦ Obviously, submission to an unbelieving husband is a little more difficult. He does not rely on God to lead him. He will make choices that do not follow God's ways, and he will have difficulty choosing to do right over choosing to follow his feelings. But even believing husbands do this at times, so the answer is always the same. **The bottom line is submitting to the Lord, and inasmuch as your husband submits to God's ways, you are able to submit to him** (1 Peter 3:1-4; Colossians 3:18).

Submission to our husbands doesn't have to be confusing or frustrating. **When we remember that God is the One we must follow and place our trust in, it's easier to give of ourselves and follow our husbands.** This is His design. And as we choose to live out His command in our daily lives, our hearts will be filled with love, joy, and peace. I pray that you will find strength to take your submission to another level without feeling as if you are "less than a woman". There's humility in submission. There's next-level in submission. There's respect and honor in submission. Don't be afraid to walk in it. Your husband will thank you for it. Believe me.

Chapter 7

LOVE

LOVE

The main thing that men desire the most is respect. The main thing that women desire is love. That's why the Bible gives specific instructions for husbands to love their wives and for wives to submit to their husbands. It's all about love and respect.

Living the fairytale dream is real. In essence, women truly just want to be loved, while men want to be honored.

Many men don't know how to love their wives according to the Word of God because they never experienced it. They came from broken homes as well. Many came without a father in the house. They were never taught or trained as to what a godly marriage is supposed to look like. How are they supposed to genuinely love their wives like Christ loves the Church?

This was something that we, my husband and I, had to tackle early on in our marriage. My husband loved me with all of his heart, but sometimes, he had a hard time showing it. He had to figure out my love language, just as I had to do his. We had to learn to embrace each other's differences and enjoy one another at all times. I had to communicate with my husband on how to love me. I had to let him know things that I liked and didn't like. I told him about things that I absolutely loved. Women, one of the biggest problems we make is "assuming" that our husbands know how to love us. Well, I came to inform you otherwise. A majority of them don't have the slightest clue. Some are close, but they still haven't quite figured it out yet. What you have to do is educate them. Tell them how you want to be loved. Tell them your likes and dislikes. Talk to them about your expectations. Don't just assume that because he's a man, he'll know. Assumptions can be some of the biggest mistakes that we make. Communication is the key. Talk to your husband about how you want to be loved in every way! Yep, I mean EVERY way! Tell him how to love you mentally, emotionally, physically, and yes, sexually! Ladies, talk to them about how you want to be made love to—your likes and dislikes! Yes, you have to educate your man. You can't assume that he already knows!

God gives a biblical foundation on how men should love their wives through the Word. It breaks it down in so many ways. Many men don't realize that the blueprint of loving a wife is written plainly in the Bible. They were never taught it that way. It was never broken down. I truly believe that it's important not just for men to know what the Word says about men loving their wives, but it's also important for the women to know as well. They need to know that anything less than that is not good! The Word is your standard. The Word is what you have as your guideline. If it's outside of the Word, then chances are, you might just have some issues in your marriage! That's just the truth! So, let's break this thing down according to the Word of God! Here are a few guidelines as to how a woman should be loved by her husband. It's like a protocol that husbands should take when trying to love their wives the RIGHT way!

Step 1: "*Love your wife as Christ loved the Church*" (Ephesians 5:25).

This means that he should be willing to risk his life to help or save his wife. Christ's love for the Church is without limits; nothing is held back. He gave His life for the Church before we loved Him. "*While we were still sinners, Christ died for us*" (Romans 5:8). His love does not depend on our love for Him; His love is unconditional. That's the same way it should be with husbands. They should have unconditional love for their wives. Under God's leadership and help, husbands can love their wives as a service, as giving their life to God. Loving his wife is to be a primary ministry of a husband, according to the word of God.

Step 2: "*Love your wife in the same way that you love your body and your life*" (Ephesians 5:28).

We care for our bodies daily. We try to be as well fed and healthy as possible. We quickly take care of any needs or desires that we may have, as well as any sexual desire as a husband should be cared for by the wife. In the same way, a husband should care for his wife's needs and well-being. He needs to feel his wife's pain and illnesses and rejoice in her health and happiness as if it were his own life. A husband must see his wife's sexual desires and make supreme efforts to meet those needs, too. Basically, her needs or desires—whether they are financial, physical, emotional, or spiritual—must receive his full attention. In this way, he can love her and provide for her, just as much as he does for himself.

Step 3: "*Husbands, in the same way be considerate as you live with your wives, and treat them with respect as the weaker partner and as heirs with you of the gracious gift of life, so that nothing will hinder your prayers*" (I Peter 3:7).

The Bible says that if husbands neglect this command, their prayers will be hindered! Yep, it's true. God takes this thing SERIOUSLY! Not loving his wife the right way can cause a husband's prayers to be hindered. The Bible tells men to be "considerate". To be considerate means to quit any irritating habits! When the wife needs to be helped with carrying heavy items etc., do it! If the wife needs time to herself, the husband should be considerate and help take care of the children for her for a bit! Men need to help their wives in any way that they can. That's what being considerate is all about. He needs to show his love to her and always be considerate of her needs and wants. It sounds simple, but a lot of men have a hard time doing it, or should I say...have a hard time at doing it consistently.

Step 4: "*Do not be harsh with your wife*" (Colossians 3:19).

I didn't say it. That's the Word of God! Women are a lot more sensitive than men, so men have to realize that harsh words, angry looks, irritated tones of voice, and impatience will deeply affect their wife. I don't believe that men understand that they can control the atmosphere in a dynamic way! Women can be the most loving, gentle and kindest people on the planet when treated right. When husbands are mean, hateful, or unloving...well, let's just say, depending on the woman, it's hard to say what type of response they'll get in return. As a woman, we love a man that's gentle and kind. With an abusive, controlling, and manipulative man, it's easy to say that there will be constant problems in the marriage until that woman decides to leave. Being gentle and kind can set a beautiful pace for a marriage to be on.

Step 5: "*The husband's body does not belong to him alone but also to his wife*" (I Corinthians 7:3-5).

A husband should have no problem with pleasing his wife physically. He should never deprive her of what she needs. Sexual pleasure is something that is given, not forced or taken. When men hold out on their wives, it stirs up insecurities and fears of him cheating, him being homosexual, or him just not being in love with the wife anymore. Either way...holding out is never a good thing for us as women, and according to the Bible, it shouldn't be done unless the two of you are in agreement about it, and even then, it should only be for a short amount of time.

Step 6: "Rejoice in your wife all your life."

Here's another step that men should take in order to love their wives according to the Word of God. "*Let her body satisfy you. Be captivated with her*" (Proverbs 5:18). No man should look at other women or pictures of other women when he has a wife on whom he can gaze daily. A husband should become fully satisfied with his wife's body, no matter what the size or shape. If a man will try and ask God to help him, he can grow to truly find his wife's body to be the most attractive in the world. This is the true spirit of being captivated with your wife. If you show that you are attracted to her, she will feel sexy and ladylike. We as women love when we get attention from our husbands. It's a blessing to know that your husband loves every inch of your body, celebrates you, enjoys you, takes care of you, and desires you. That's one of the ways that women truly feel loved by their spouses.

Step 7: "*Women may be dressed in simple clothing, with a quiet and serious air; not with vanity about her hair and gold or jewels or expensive clothing,*" (1 Timothy 2:9). A husband should encourage his wife to be modest in public and erotic in private.

A modest woman is a lady. There is so much sin and temptation that results from women showing too much skin in public. Women, we can be SEXY without being worldly sexy. Worldly sexy makes you want to show everything just because it's "the thing to do". Just think of the pleasure of knowing that no one sees too much of your legs but your husband! Your breasts, your thighs…they belong to him. I'm not saying you can't put on a little sexy black dress showing your curves. I'm saying don't put on something that will make you look just like the girl on the corner. The lady in the house is classy, chic, fabulous, and, oh, so sexy! She can give her husband the "girl on the corner" vibes strictly in the comfort of their own home, in their private sanctuary! A real lady knows how to be both but has the wisdom on when to be both!

Step 8: "*Do not be captivated by other women*" (Proverbs 5:20).

Finding other women attractive and looking at them will degrade a man's view of his own wife because he will start to compare her with them. He will be less satisfied with her, and she will feel less special to him. No man can build a habit of glances without subconsciously doing it in his wife's company, and she will definitely notice and be hurt. A husband needs to always remember to be captivated with his own wife and no one else. She will feel like the queen of the world and will fall more and more in love with him.

Step 9: "*Call your wife 'blessed' and praise her*" (Proverbs 31:28-29).

A man should tell his wife that she is special and that she is greater than any other woman on earth. He shouldn't just mention her physical beauty, but compliment her on her care for him, her hard work and her ladylike attributes. Constantly filling the wife's heart with praise will cause her to blossom in so many ways. She longs for those words, and she wants to hear them from her husband! A wife needs and longs to be treasured by her husband. This will not lead to a prideful woman; it will lead to a woman who feels loved for who she is.

Step 10: "*Tell your wife how captivated you are with her*" (Song of Songs 4:7, 7:1-8)

A true lover will make sure that his wife knows he finds no flaw in her. God made the wife, and God makes no mistakes. If a man finds a part of her flawed, physically or in her personality, then it is his mind that needs to be changed. The responsibility upon the man to grow to love and to express love for every part of his wife is needed. Also, respectfully and sensually, he needs to tell her so. It will not help to criticize her or to be sarcastic. If he does this, it will probably result in her wanting to be less romantic with him less often. A wife will feel amazing when she knows that her husband is captivated with her.

Step 11: "*Honor your marriage; keep it pure by remaining true to your wife in every way*" (Hebrews 13:4).

Jesus says that "lustful looks are adultery" (Matthew 5:28). This is similar to "where your treasure is, there will your heart be also"(Luke 12:34). Men should not treasure such lust in any area of life. They should deny it access to their heart. They can keep their marriage pure by training their heart and eyes to be true to their wives. Marriages will reap huge benefits if this is done and will hopefully last for a lifetime!

Step 12: "*Be thankful for your wife and realize the favor you have received from God*" (Proverbs 18:22).

A man would be truly lonely without a wife. Adam was alone, and it wasn't good for him to be alone, so God gave him a wife. When God gives a wife, He gives a lifetime companion, a friend, and a lover to enjoy every day. What a blessing! Men should thank God and pray for their wives daily. They are a tremendous "prize" from God.

Step 13: "*Be one flesh with your wife in every way*" (Matthew 19:5).

A husband should enjoy life with his wife as if he wants to be inseparable from her. He should long to be with her, think about her during the day, call her every day, and text her as much as he can. Learn as a couple how to agree or agree to disagree on everything and be like-minded. Enjoy intimacy and sex often. You should have sex as often as is necessary to meet the desires of whichever spouse has the stronger sex drive and as schedules and health permit. Spend time just talking and sharing the day's events. Show a genuine interest and listen intently to each other. It's important that a husband gives his wife full attention and eye contact any time she is talking to him. The wife should be more important than anything or anyone but Jesus Christ.

Step 14: Be patient and kind. No bragging, no competition. You are one.

1 Corinthians 13:4-7 states, *"Love is patient, love is kind. It does not envy, it does not boast, it is not proud. It does not dishonor others, it is not self-seeking, it is not easily angered, it keeps no record of wrongs. Love does not delight in evil but rejoices with the truth. It always protects, always trusts, always hopes, always perseveres."*

Step 15: Love as a way of life.
Some say love is an act of benevolence. That is not totally true. People can do a beneficial action with an unloving attitude. The husband who says with a harsh voice, "Okay, I'll take the garbage out if you will get off my back," has not performed an act of love. The husband who mows the grass simply because his wife has been nagging him for weeks is doing a kind act, but it may be done to silence her critical words. The wife who agrees to be sexually intimate with her husband simply out of a sense of duty or guilt is not performing an act of love, either. Love is the choice to cooperate with God in serving your spouse. The individuals who truly love see themselves as God's agents for enriching the lives of their marriage partner. For them, love is a way of life. They are constantly looking for ways to help, encourage and support their spouse. Such love often stimulates warm, romantic feelings in the heart of the spouse. Emotions are the icing on the cake, but without a loving attitude and appropriate behavior, the icing will melt.

Learning how to love your spouse should be a classroom that you sit in every day, studying how to master the test. It's a lifestyle. It should be something practiced every single day of our lives.

Chapter 8

Money, Money, MONEY

Money, Money, MONEY

It's the money issue....so where do I begin? Hmm...let's see. Marriage and finances...

Money has been one of the top reasons that couples get divorced. According to marriage.com, it's the number-two reason behind the number-one reason: infidelity.

Money makes people funny, or so the saying goes, and it's true.

Everything from different spending habits and financial goals to one spouse making considerably more money than the other (causing a power struggle) can strain a marriage to the breaking point. "Money really touches everything. It impacts people's lives," said Emmet Burns, brand marketing director for SunTrust. "Clearly, money and stress do seem to go hand in hand for many couples. Financial troubles can be categorized as one of the biggest causes of divorce, following infidelity, the number-one reason for divorce."

As the saying goes also...money runs the world, but in many cases, money can run and ruin a marriage. It can be a divisive mechanism IF you allow it. The Bible tells us in 1 Timothy 6:10 NIV that *"For the love of money is a root of all kinds of evil. Some people, eager for money, have wandered from the faith and pierced themselves with many griefs."* However, I LOVE The Message version of this scripture: *"9-10But if it's only money these leaders are after, they'll self-destruct in no time. Lust for money brings trouble and nothing but trouble. Going down that path, some lose their footing in the faith completely and live to regret it bitterly ever after."*

So, let me say it in a way that correlates with The Message version but in a way that's directed towards marriage: If it's money that your marriage is based on, then it'll self-destruct or be destroyed in no time. Whether you and your spouse have a lot of money or a little, it should not dictate how long you will be married. Whether you're broke or rich, your love for one another should ALWAYS outweigh your love for money! If you desire money more than your marriage, it will always bring nothing but trouble, heartache, and pain. You lose sight of what's more important, and it will cause you to go down a path that God never intended for you to go on. You will end up regretting your decision later, once you become more mature and seasoned.

I have questions that I want you to think about while reading this chapter— questions that I will address, of course, but think about this as you read through this chapter.

How is it that money can divide a house so easily? How is it that married couples can live more like roommates than as a couple united together in marriage? How is it that you "split" bills with your spouse? How is it that you will let your "spouse" borrow money from you? How is it that a married couple have separate or secret accounts? How is it that if you don't have enough money, you have MAJOR problems in your marriage? How is it that if the money "don't stop acting funny", then your marriage is good as gone?

When you divide the bills, you divide your house. When you divide your money, you divide your house. When you act like two instead of one, then division has taken place somewhere. When you treat your spouse like someone in your family trying to borrow money from you, then you have just divided your house. How is it that when two becomes one, you still act like you're two? What exactly happens when you divide your house financially?

I know many may not want to hear this, but I have to give you truth. I have to talk about the error that I see in marriages that spills over into major issues that lead them straight to divorce court! However, in talking about these issues, I have to give you what the Word says about it. So, exactly what does the Word say about a divided house? Well, I'm certainly glad you asked!

No matter what, if you divide your house in any way, that house will not be able to stand.

Mark 3:25 New International Version:
"If a house is divided against itself, that house cannot stand."

If your finances are divided, your finances will also divide your house. When YOUR

FINANCES divide the house, it will fall if you don't figure out a way to unite and become one even in that area of your life.

Mark 10:8 Amplified Bible (AMP):

"And the two shall become one flesh; so that they are no longer two, but [are united as] one flesh."

Wow. Two becoming one. The Bible truly makes it plain. The question is can we accept the fact that our marriage should be unified even when it comes to finances? Check out The Message version of this same scripture.

Mark 10:8-9 The Message (MSG):

Jesus said, "Moses wrote this command only as a concession to your hardhearted ways. In the original creation, God made male and female to be together. Because of this, a man leaves father and mother, and in marriage he becomes one flesh with a woman—no longer two individuals, but forming a new unity. Because God created this organic union of the two sexes, no one should desecrate his art by cutting them apart."

In this scripture, it takes us back to the original creation with Adam and Eve. Imagine this. What if Adam told Eve, "Eve, I'll go out and till the ground. I'll get food to eat. You go out till the ground, too. You get food as well to provide for the house. What I get is mine. What you get is yours. We can share certain things at certain times, but when it comes to what we get from the work we do, it has to be divided. Now listen, Eve. If you run out, I'll let you borrow some of mine, but you must pay me back. If I have more than enough, you may not have to pay me back. It just depends on what I got in the stash for that week. Eve, other than that, you go get yours. I'll go get mine. I'll put my half in. You put your half in. We're good. If you need to borrow from me...let me know. I'll try to help you as much as I can."

I'm not trying to be funny, but I am giving you a harsh reality of what today's marriages look like. They set up a way out at the beginning of the marriage, you know...kind of like celebrities. They have millions in the bank. When they get married, they want to hold on to those millions and not completely share them with the one that they supposedly became "one" with. So, what do they do? They set up prenuptial agreements. This agreement is designed to set up a great division within the marriage so that if something happens, you're not getting anything from me. They set themselves up for division before they are even married. They go in with the mindset that what's mine is mine, and what's theirs is theirs. They will not unite in this area, and when they get tired of each other, they have already established their way out.

How many people go into a marriage believing that it will fail? Many people marry nowadays for the convenience, not the longevity. The longevity of it all says that I'm in it for the long haul. The convenience of it all says that it's meeting a need for this moment in your life.

When my husband and I married, we were not rich. As a matter of fact, we were young, dumb, and stupid when it came to money. We didn't have a lot of money. We had major financial struggles when we first got married; however, one thing that I can truly say is that those financial struggles NEVER had us. We purposed in our hearts to never let financial issues come between us. When we got married, we established all of our accounts TOGETHER. We had checking and savings accounts. We knew that we wanted to save and get to another level, even though we didn't know how to save for real. We eventually learned along the way. You see, our families never taught us the type of relationship that we should have with money. We never learned how to save, how to invest, how to budget, etc. That was not something that our parents taught us. We had to learn for ourselves. We did see our parents walking in oneness when it came to finances, though. My dad brought his check home every week and gave it to my mom. She would cash it, put some in the bank, pay the bills and take care of the home. It was always the natural thing to do. My dad was a great provider. He made sure that he worked hard to take good care of our family. He made sure we had what we needed and, many times, what we wanted. My family never took a house-divided approach until my mom eventually divorced my dad. As stated earlier, my dad had several counts of infidelity, which created a DIVIDED house for him and my mom. She was loyal and faithful to one man. He lived a divided life, having other women involved. And we know what the scripture says about a divided house; it will always fall, no matter where the division is coming from! But of course, in this chapter, our focus in on the finances, so let's stay there.

So, as you can see, my husband and I grew up with a traditional mindset when it came to finances. We would be unified in that area. I didn't marry my husband for money, so money most certainly was NOT going to tear us apart. With everything I have, I am always willing to give it to him. With everything he has, he will give to me as well. There are no limits in our relationship. Everything we got, we got together. Our financial goals, we got them together. We talk about savings, investing, budgeting, etc. We make sure we are on one accord trying to reach the same goal of getting to the top of the mountain together, no matter who brings in the most money. We are in this thing TOGETHER!

Anytime we have to make a large purchase, we discuss it. We discuss where we are and where we are headed financially. I must say, I am the "spender". My husband is far more conservative. He would save every dime if I let him. I tell him that we DO want to live a little bit, too! Everything can't be saved!

My husband actually helped me to see the value in saving. I didn't get it at first. I always had the mindset that we can't take it with us when we're dead and gone, so why not spend it all! Yeah, I know. It's not right! Listen, this was my mindset at the beginning of my marriage. Like I said…I was young, dumb, and stupid when it came to finances. I'm so happy to say that I have grown tremendously in this area. I needed to get on one accord with my husband. I had to realize my weaknesses (shopping, shoes, clothes…anything in the fashion realm). I had to do something about it. I made a decision that I would be a student of business, money, and finances. I continue to grow every day in this area by surrounding myself with the right people to help me be wise and a good steward when it comes to finances. I also know that I want my family to go to another level as well. So, my husband and I work hard at being good stewards over our finances. We understand that we can have so much more together than we ever could apart. Dividing our finances would never be an option.

So, what are some solutions if you have separate accounts and are trying to become one in your finances? Discuss your financial goals together. What do you want to save? What monies are you willing to invest? What are your priorities when paying bills? It's okay to have different accounts for different things, but it should be done on one accord together. What exactly do I mean by that? Here are some suggestions for having your accounts together as one. This means that both of you have access to them. Both of your names are on those accounts (unity), even if it's for the other spouse. That means that if my husband sets up an account for me for free spending, meaning I can spend it however I want (almost like we set up allowance accounts for each other) both of our names are on it (unity), but it's designated for that one person to spend how they want. We both can make deposits into it, but we are on one accord that it's for that particular spouse to spend. We know what goes in it. We know when it gets low. We can both deposit back into the account if necessary because we both have access to it. So again, here are some account suggestions to have as a married couple that you can both sign your names to:

1) Checking
2) Savings
3) Investment
4) Emergency
5) Spending (husband)
6) Spending (wife)
7) Savings (children)
8) College fund
9) Retirement

I want to give you 10 great reasons why marriages should share finances. I really believe this will help you out:

1. You are one when you're married, so you are one with money, too!

The whole purpose of marriage is that you now are one. Married couples are found to be more dissatisfied when they don't pool their finances, and couples who pool at least 80% of their income are happier than couples who pool 70% or less. This stuff matters.

2. Sharing finances means you've jumped "all in" to the marriage.

When people hold back their money, it's almost as if they're holding back part of themselves. It's like we're saying, "I need this money in case our marriage doesn't work," or "I'm holding on to this because I need to still have independence."

If you're worried the marriage won't work or if you still need independence, *you shouldn't have gotten married.*

And studies have repeatedly shown that couples who fully commit create love and a good marriage. The simple act of commitment often makes people act more lovingly because they know they're in this for life. So, don't hold back!

3. Total transparency comes from shared finances, not split finances.

Marriage means total transparency. You shouldn't be keeping things from each other because that builds distance. If you don't know about your spouse's financial situation, that's not good for your marriage. Besides it can be dangerous if one of you is ever incapacitated or hurt and the other needs access quickly.

4. If you share finances, you don't have to keep track of "his" and "hers" expenses.

I heard of a couple who keeps completely separate finances. They even have a "his" car and a "her" car. But this can lead to needless stress over the smallest of things. For instance, they got in a squabble once when his car was in the garage, but they had to take a four-hour drive out of town because his family was having a reunion, so they took her car. But when it came to gas, who should pay? He said it was *her* car; she said it was *his* family. I listened, flabbergasted, because I can't imagine ever having to negotiate this stuff since everything Derrick and I have ever had is "ours". And thus, we avoid these squabbles entirely.

5. Sharing finances allows you to budget easily.

When you share finances, you have something called a "household income". You can then look at that number and decide together what your spending should be. If, on the other hand, you each keep separate finances and contribute a certain amount into a pool every month or divide up the bills to be paid, then it's much harder to keep a lid on spending and make some long-term goals. Incidentally, having a "household income" does not mean that you can't allocate money for you to spend as you see fit. Decide what needs to go where. I mentioned earlier the different types of accounts that can be established once you have your sit-down with your spouse in regards to your finances.

6. Sharing finances allows you to make retirement goals.

One day neither of you will be working, and retirement savings need to be coordinated. How much do we need together? For tax purposes, who should have the most in a 401K? If you are each contributing for retirement separately, it's much harder to coordinate these goals. And the one who is more of a saver could easily resent the one who is more of a spender and isn't contributing as much. When you have a household budget that includes a line for "retirement savings," this is much easier to negotiate, which is probably why couples who share finances tend to save more!

7. Sharing finances allows you to save for short-term goals.

Let's not just look at the long-term, though. What if you decide that it would be really nice to take the family on a cruise in two years? How do you budget for that? Do you each have to contribute equally? What if it's more important to one than the other? Again, when you share finances and have a shared budget, these decisions are easier to make.

8. If you share finances, you get a heads-up if someone's in trouble.

What if someone has a gambling problem or a spending problem? What if someone is doing something they shouldn't be doing and leading a double life? It's much harder for these things to become issues if the finances are shared and open. And when being secretive isn't that easy, it often takes away the temptation for many of these things which could all too easily become addictions. It's just accountability…and it works!

9. Sharing finances means there's not an automatic spirit of "doing your share".

When you're splitting finances, there's this underlying assumption that you each should "do your share". That leads to a dynamic where the goal is "fairness". Any time in a marriage where you're trying to measure if someone is doing their share, there will be tension because people tend to value their own efforts more. If she earns more money, does that mean that she only has to contribute the same amount he makes, and she can keep the rest? If he gets a raise, does he have to share it with her? If he's working overtime, should she have to work overtime too? If she goes back to work, does childcare have to completely come out of her income?

If you're always trying to keep things fair, then the focus will always be on what is right for me, rather than what is right for the family.

10. Sharing marriage finances leads to a family focus, not a self-focus.

I know a couple who, when they got married, assumed that they would each contribute a certain amount of money to the household each month.

But then she got pregnant, and somehow the expectation that she should keep contributing money didn't go away. He didn't suddenly start paying "her" bills (the ones they had allotted to her, like electricity) just because she had just delivered a baby. So, when the baby was very young, she had Grandma baby-sit and went back to work. Meanwhile, he was spending a lot of money on fishing trips because he was still contributing "his share".

Ecclesiastes 4:9-10 says:

> *Two are better than one*
> *because they have a good return for their labor:*
> *If either of them falls down,*
>   *one can help the other up.*
> *but pity anyone who falls*
>   *and has no one to help them up.*

One of the benefits of marriage is that someone has our back! If one person goes through a period of unemployment, the other steps in and helps. If one is sick (or just delivered a baby!), the other one covers. In fact, "specialization" is one of the things that brings the most happiness and satisfaction to married couples vs. unmarried couples. When you are totally committed and "all-in" to the relationship, then you can each start to do what you do best, rather than having to act the same way you did before you were married. So, if one makes more money, they can work more while the other is home with the kids, and it works out better for everyone.

When you're married, you're not roommates splitting the bills for the common cause of having a place to stay. If I wanted a roommate, I could have stayed single. I want someone that I can become one with every single day of my life and in every aspect of my life. Nothing, not even money, should create a divided house. And when you realize that something is creating a divided house, it's up to you and your spouse to get it right.

So why is putting monies together as one such an issue? Why is this so hard for many couples to do? Let me break this down based on some things that I have seen with couples throughout the years of counseling them.

1. Fear
2. Control

3. Secret lives
4. Deception
5. Pride
6. Rebellion

Fear

One thing that I have noticed with many couples (though they may not come out and say it exactly) is that they are fearful of putting their monies together. Having separate accounts gives them more peace about their finances. One may be afraid of the other's spending habits. This could be something as simple as them thinking they spend too much money on clothes and shoes or some other thing that they may feel is fruitless. In cases like this, there is a simple fix. This is where you have to sit down and discuss financial goals and priorities. This is where you teach each other how to be on one accord when it comes to the finances. You have to communicate expectations, goals, likes, dislikes, etc. You can't just assume that your spouse knows what you want to achieve financially. You have to figure out a way to make your goal and their goal one. This will include compromise, swallowing your pride and looking at the big picture of what it's going to take to make sure that your house prospers in the area of finances. When you get on one page financially, you'll be able to achieve so much more than you could ever achieve independently.

Now there are other "special" situations that could stir up fear when it comes to finances in the marriage. You may have to make a special exception for this one, especially when it brings your house to an extremely low place! Take, for example, someone that is married to an addict. This addict may be addicted to drugs, alcohol, gambling, etc. With this addiction, it causes the spouse to spend money that was intended for food, clothing, shelter, bills, etc. With it being an extreme case, you may have to establish a separate account to stow away money so that you can use it to pay bills. Often times, addicts will use and take anything just so they can get their "fix". They'll sacrifice their family's well-being to do that. It's sad, but it happens. Until that spouse is healed, set free and delivered, establishing another account may be your only option. This is what I call a "special case situation"; however, you still have to remember the foundation of the Word in regards to a divided house. At some point or another, it will fall if you don't get it unified, even in cases like this.

That's why it's super important to figure out how you and your spouse can get on one accord with finances. It will make your life so much easier. If you have to fast and pray- fast and pray to get past any issues that hinder your house (such as addictions); fast and pray until you see what you are believing God for.

When you love money more than you love your family, when you put money before your family, when you allow money to divide your family, you just allowed "the love of money" to be the root (one of the roots) to evil manifesting in your marriage. Don't fear. Trust God. Trust that even in this area, it will work for your good if you let it.

Control

Control is another major factor in why families can't be unified in their marriages when it comes to finances. The idea of having control over your own finances and not coming into oneness with your spouse is significant. Many think that if they gave over that control, they may lose what they have. They think they lose their say. They think they lose their power. Then, the love for money begins to take over their mindset. They love money so much that they refuse to give over the control they have to someone else. Sharing control over money is not an option for them. Control brings power. Control brings ownership. Having control allows them to not fear losing it to someone else. When it's all said and done, if something ever happened in their marriage, they already have control over their finances, so the other party doesn't really know how much they have in the bank, and it's easier to deceive the other because you never give them control over your finances to know what you have and don't have.

For many, losing control over their finances shows weakness and vulnerability. Many don't want to trust their spouse to that extent and give them shared control when it comes to finances. That's where the "let's act more like roommates than married people" comes in. With a roommate, you control your part, and they control theirs. As long as everyone is controlling "their part," things should be good, right? Wrong. So many marriages with separate accounts have more financial issues when they fail to have shared control/shared finances with their spouses. Losing control shows that you are willing to be vulnerable and trust the one that God has given to you with EVERYTHING. That includes finances.

Secret Lives

When you don't have shared finances, it's easier to have secrets. It's easier to have NO accountability whatsoever when it comes to money. Your spouse doesn't know what you're spending or how you're spending it. They have no say so. The only concern is that the "part you pay" comes through.

It's easier to have a secret life when there's no accountability. I was listening to a story that had made major news of how a husband (who made really good money and had his own stash for himself) had another family living five minutes from where his family lived. He was taking care of two homes, and his wife had no clue. All she knew was that the bills were paid, and they were well taken care of in their homes. Now, if she could have had access to his accounts, seen the bank statements, and knew what was going on in the bank, more than likely, her husband wouldn't have gotten away with it for as long as he did.

This is seriously a trick of the enemy to divide homes when it comes to finances. It's easier to have secret lives when there is no accountability. It's easier to waste money and pay for hotels, strip clubs, drugs, alcohol, etc., when your income is not accounted for with the family.

Now, I'm not stating that everyone that has separate accounts has a secret life. Nope. I'm saying it's easier for it to happen when there's no accountability for finances.

Being on one accord when it comes to finances can bring so much peace and unity within the home. It breaks down the wall of selfishness. It promotes unity. It takes away division. It helps a family to avoid having "secret lives" because the money is shared, and their finances are accounted for...on one accord!

Deception

Deception is *"the act of deceiving, the state of being deceived; something that deceives or is intended to deceive; fraud."* To deceive is *"to mislead by a false appearance or statement; delude; to be unfaithful to (one's spouse); to mislead or falsely persuade others; practice deceit"* (dictionary.com).

Many people are afraid of joining incomes because they are afraid that their spouse will know the truth about them, about their finances, about their life. Deception and secret lives can go hand in hand because to live a secret life is to deceive your spouse; however, deception is not just about living a secret life. There are many couples who don't want their spouse to know how much money they make, so they deceive the other into thinking that it's one thing when it's really more, or sometimes even less, than what they said.

They also may not want their spouse to know about certain bills that they may have, hobbies that they keep or places that they may frequent (e.g. strip clubs, bars, hotels, etc.). They use deception so that their spouse is ignorant to what's really going on.

Deception never goes well. Sooner or later, what's in the dark will come to light. When these secret things are revealed to that particular spouse, it never goes well for that marriage. It divides the house in such a way that divorce becomes the only option. That's one of the reasons why money is the second leading cause of divorces. A divided house, a house that walks in deception, always falls and leads to destruction.

Pride

The dark side of pride sows the seed for the weeds of conflict to take root and spread throughout a marriage. When it comes to money issues in a marriage, one spouse will be all about "me and mine" and will refuse to come together as one when it comes to finances. They like doing their own thing with little accountability. They like doing things their own way. It's more about them than anything else. Without realizing it, they walk in pride and selfishness without having a true understanding of how it may be affecting their household. The Bible says that "*Pride only breeds quarrels*" (Proverbs 13:10a). If pride is left unchecked, it can eventually lead to an absolute loss of intimacy, communication and connection between a husband and wife. Ultimately, its tendrils can choke the life out of a marriage and cause the end of the marriage. As King Solomon wrote, "*Pride goes before destruction, a haughty spirit before a fall*" (Proverbs 16:18).

- Pride is revealed in an "I'm right and you're wrong" theme in a relationship.
- Pride is demonstrated in verbal cuts and put-downs to elevate or set apart the aggressor.

- Pride is a driver of entitlement. It reveals an "I don't deserve this, so I deserve to be compensated with that."
- Pride is centered on self and rarely serves another unless there is self-interest involved (i.e. "If I'm nice today, perhaps we can make love tonight," or "If I say nice things, perhaps I can purchase this," or "It's my money, I do what I want to.")

Humility is the anti-pride. The apostle Paul wrote, "*Do nothing out of selfish ambition or vain conceit, but in humility consider others better than yourselves*" (Philippians 2:3). In a marriage, it's so important to set aside pride and ego, especially when it comes to the finances. One has to realize that the picture is much bigger than them. When they realize that the family needs to be one and not isolated, then they will realize that they can have so much more together than they ever will with divided finances.

Rebellion

Rebellion is all about resistance. Resistance to control or tradition is how dictionary.com describes it. In a marriage and in regards to finances, one spouse might rebel against having joint accounts because they don't like sharing control over their money. Their money is their money, right?

Many who rebel when it comes to finances do things such as buying things that their spouse is not in agreement with. If they want it, and they have the money to get it, then who can tell them otherwise? In essence, they end up rebelling against the principle of being one, even when it comes to finances. If a spouse can't handle having shared control in regards to their finances, they typically do things to rebel. This could be anything from getting an attitude when finances are discussed, buying things that the other may not agree with, setting up prenuptial agreements in regards to having unified monies (this is rebellion against the tradition of being on one according to the Word of God), having secret accounts, or being dishonest about finances. The reality is all of the things that we previously discussed are included in this category. This just means that one spouse will bring opposition to the idea of being one when it comes to finances. They don't want it, so they do things to rebel against it.

Conclusion

Loving your spouse more than you love money is rather important. It's not about who's making more. It's not about what's in it for me. It's not about having secret lives. It's about being committed to one another, so much so that you will NOT let anything divide you, including money.

Marriage is about unity, love, and harmony. It's about being on one accord with everything, learning to agree to disagree, and being able to compromise. It's about humility and joy; it's about doing whatever is necessary to ensure that you live a long and strong life TOGETHER. No division, but one accord. It's about choosing to take away any form of division so that you are able to walk together on one accord, trusting each other not just with your money, but with your life! What God has joined together, you have to make sure no one (including yourselves) or nothing (including money) separates or divides your marriage in any way, shape, fashion, or form. You have to choose to get over yourself, your independence and your ways so that you can learn how to walk in peace, love, joy, and harmony with the one that God gave you to be with. Your marriage is much bigger than money. Remember that.

Chapter 9

Let's Talk About **SEX**, Baby!

LET'S TALK ABOUT SEX, BABY!

Questions from a FRUSTRATED husband:

"How can a couple resolve arguments over how often to have sex? I'm frustrated because my wife would probably be content to make love once a month, which doesn't come close to satisfying me. Is she abnormal, or am I some kind of pervert? Is there any way to resolve this conflict?"

She says: "But we were intimate just last Wednesday."

He says: "Honey, that was three Wednesdays ago."

These days, the common complaint is "not often enough."

But then again, look who's complaining. Do husbands feel deprived because of their wives' unwillingness to be intimate, or are women feeling the pressure about doing their wifely duty in addition to laundry, cooking, driving, disciplining, attending school meetings, and grocery shopping?

Even the Bible or New Testament states that sex should not be denied or demanded. If one spouse does not feel like having sex, the other spouse must respect that. It goes the other way, too; if one spouse likes to have sex, then the other spouse must agree. Sexual compromise is strongly encouraged, provided it is reasonable.

Sex is a very important component in the marriage. It's something that establishes intimacy to an even greater level. Where there's no sex, often there are problems. Sometimes the problems are unspoken but eventually get revealed through the frustrations of one of the spouses.

There are so many reasons why sex and intimacy are essential for a married couple. The benefits of good sex and intimate moments are profound both for the spouses and for the marriage they share together. Even if it's busy around the household, good sex should never be put at the bottom of the list of your priorities. Here are a few reasons why:

It's the tie that binds.

If a married couple can achieve deep emotional and sexual intimacy, their marriage can surely thrive on for many years ahead. Let us differentiate the two.

Emotional intimacy is the kind of intimacy that two sincere friends can share with each other. It is likely to be very stable and can last a lifetime. For us to achieve a healthy level of emotional intimacy, we have to be able to share honest, open and genuine communication. It is from this intimacy that we gain strength and develop confidence in our relationship because we can share our most profound and most important thoughts and feelings with our partner.

Sexual intimacy, on the other hand, is the kind of intimacy in which our bodies are communicating. When we think about sexual intimacy, we often think about the sexual acts that involve touching, feeling each other's genitals and penetrative sex. But it goes far beyond that. **Good sex involves the chemistry of emotional intimacy and sexual intimacy. They both have to work together for the sex to be considered "good".** When the marriage is new, the sexual drive is commonly high, and the freedom to have sex is available. This is what we call the "honeymoon phase".

When this phase is over, some couples can fall into a rut. They turn away from focusing on the intimacy and communication that they once had; they might turn away from each other sexually. Sexual problems then may arise.

Fights about the stagnancy that is now happening in the couple's sex life may put the couple against each other, and then the blame game starts. At these crucial moments, emotional intimacy comes in. If you have achieved a level of emotional intimacy with your spouse and there is trust in your spouse that you will be heard, you can discuss even the most sensitive issues such as your sex lives. Emotional intimacy empowers you to be able to speak about your needs without being ashamed of having them.

This is similar to being able to share with your doctor your health problems and trusting that whatever you share with them will be held in confidentiality and that you will be receiving the best treatment following their diagnosis. Emotional intimacy should allow you to do the same. Good sex cannot be achieved without the intimacy shared between you and your partner. It's almost cyclical that the more you are open with your partner, the more good sex you'll have and the more your relationship can get stronger overall.

Relationship thermometer

If you are a newlywed couple and you are not having as much good sex as you are expecting, there might be some issues that you might need to address.

For a couple to be able to have good sex, knowing how to have sex isn't enough; it's also about sharing the open intimacy between each other and being able to communicate well with your partner, especially when it comes to discussing your needs. This process allows you to share sexual intimacy as well. By assessing how intimate you are and whether you are enjoying good communication and good sex, you can understand the temperature of your relationship, which means you can be alerted to problems so that you can resolve them quickly if the temperature cools down.

One of the aspects that you can quickly check within your relationship is your communication. Are you letting your spouse speak about their needs, their desires and their fantasies without being judged? If so, congratulations! You are opening the table for a healthy discussion on sex. If you can share these kinds of conversations, you are well on your way to a lifetime of strong intimacy levels. Talking about a sensitive topic such as sex can prove to be a mountain to climb, but if you and your spouse have open and non-judgmental communication, what once was a mountain can now become a lowland to traverse.

Improved quality of life

Having good sex improves your quality of life. With increased sexual activity, you are increasing your shared moments of intimacy with your partner. And not only that, having regular sex increases your body's production of the feel-good hormones, thereby making you feel empowered and more confident. It also helps in making you happy!

Aside from the feel-good hormones that this intimate activity gives, sex is proven to improve overall physical health. In general, regular sex improves your immune function. It helps you fight off viruses better. And not only that, but it also helps improve your quality of sleep! And who doesn't want better sleep?

Sex also has specific benefits for husbands and wives. For males, those who partake in regular sexual activity had lower risks of developing prostate cancer. For the females, it was observed that regular orgasms helped in strengthening the pelvic floor, and it was also reported that they experienced lesser pains when they were menstruating. Yesss! Get it, ladies! ☺

Overall, there is not a bad thing that can be said about having sex with your spouse. The more intimate you are with your spouse, the better sex you'll have, the more sex you'll have and the better your relationship will be! I would like to focus on the fact that it's not always about the quantity but the quality. However, if you have found yourselves stuck in a rut, it will help to have an open conversation about your intimacy situation with your spouse. If speaking about the situation scares you, it might be best to go to therapy to facilitate the conversation. If your spouse suddenly opens up to you and says "I'm bored" with our sex life, do not panic. It's okay. This is emotional intimacy. This is the type of conversation that needs to be had in order for your sex life to go to another level, especially if you have been married for a long time and feel like something new needs to happen. It's time to start thinking of some new sex ideas to try.

Here are a few amazing sex ideas to try with your spouse tonight. It'll work…if you work it! 😊

1. Seduce your spouse

Whether you're the husband or the wife, SEDUCE your spouse tonight!

Ladies, it's important to know that your husbands are highly visual creatures. Their sense of sight is easily stimulated. What better way to use this knowledge than to walk around in your sexiest lingerie (or if you prefer, your birthday suit) and seduce your spouse. If you're not feeling confident about your body, do not fret. Most women claim that wearing the right lingerie made them feel good and confident. The key is in finding the right lingerie that will drive him crazy and make you feel fabulous too. Embrace your natural, feminine sexuality, ladies! Your spouse will be delighted that you did!

Gentlemen, you are not being asked to perform a dance routine, e.g. Magic Mike, when seducing your spouse, and you are not expected to! (Although, there could be some bonus points if you do show off your dance moves.) To seduce your wife, you must know what makes her tick. After being in a relationship for so long, it could be assumed that you have gotten to know your wife down to her most intimate quirk. If your wife has been giving you "excuses" for not having sex, maybe it's time to help her out by asking her how you can help her relax (remember seduction can start outside of the bedroom!).

2. Food Teasers

Have you heard of aphrodisiacs? In the world of food, aphrodisiacs are food items that are thought to increase your sexual appetite. Some of the well-known aphrodisiacs are easily accessible, such as a bar of dark chocolate, wine, and oysters. However, if you are not fond of any of these previously mentioned food items, you can still incorporate food in your sexy time!

When we were young, we were all taught not to play with our food, but we're all adults now! So, let's break some rules! One of the classic food items that you can include is whipped cream. Put some whipped cream on the body of your spouse and lick away. You can do this with other similar items such as syrup or honey.

3. Talk dirty

You and your spouse's exchange of messages right now may be all about buying groceries, reminders on chores or a few "I love yous" here and there, but when it comes to sex talk, it can be drier than the Sahara Desert! Sext your spouse. Sending naughty texts to your spouse can form part of your foreplay session in preparation for an evening of action. If you are not the type to send sexts, however, flirt with your spouse instead. Tell your husband how handsome he is today, tell him what you want to do to him, allow your mouth to be filled with things that excite him, that stir him up, that have him on edge about coming home to you! Let him know what's waiting for him when he comes home. I guarantee you; he'll try to get off of work early!

4. Get ready to play

Sexual fantasies are natural, just as much as winning the lottery and buying a house as a fantasy is natural. Fantasies may not be part of your everyday talk, but as partners, it may be beneficial to talk about each other's fantasies and maybe even live them out! While it may be awkward to have this talk with your spouse, it may be worth it in the end. The most common fantasy among men is to give their woman multiple orgasms. For this fantasy to be lived out, it's best for the wife to know what turns them on and what makes them orgasm. The information shared with your spouse will not only bring you closer together, but will help you live out such a fantasy.

FOREPLAY MATTERS!

Before you start the car, you have to "turn on" on the engine! Foreplay is a big deal, especially for women. Rolling over and getting on top of a woman for the sake of "let me have an orgasm"…let's just say it doesn't go over too well for most women. Taking the time to let things heat up can be the key to having the ultimate satisfaction for you and your spouse in the bedroom. Whoever said the most important thing in life is to finish strong never had a frank conversation with a woman about the importance of foreplay. When it comes to sexual prelude, men and women don't always see eye to eye.

According to WebMD, "It's particularly important for women to have successful foreplay because it takes a woman a longer time [than a man] to get up to the level of arousal needed to orgasm," says "Dr. Ruth" Westheimer, EdD, a psychosexual therapist, professor at New York University, and lecturer at Yale and Princeton Universities.

A man can just think about sex and have an erection, but for most women, wanting sex is not enough, says Westheimer. Foreplay serves a physical and emotional purpose, helping prepare both the mind and body for sex. Many women need to be kissed, hugged, and caressed to create lubrication in the vagina, which is important for comfortable intercourse."

Here are 7 important things to know about foreplay:

1. Treat it like an appetizer and always order one

Too often, couples forgo foreplay altogether and speed ahead to intercourse, and in doing so, they may be setting themselves up for failure. When it comes to eating, lots of people like to skip the appetizer. That's fine for food, but skipping foreplay is rarely a good idea for sex. The right foreplay can send you from 0 to 1,000 on the horniness scale. Let's just be real. You won't be able to drive the car unless you press the button—the right button to start it!

2. Foreplay and sexual satisfaction go hand-in-hand, especially for women

It's a fact: Women typically need foreplay to have good sex. That's a really good reason not to cut corners with it. Foreplay is really important for most women because we tend to take a longer time to get into the mood. Usually it's women who complain that men want to skip to the main course of intercourse, but often we need more time to open up. Foreplay helps lubrication flow and makes intercourse all the more pleasurable.

3. Sensuality is the secret to great foreplay

Sensuality is key—holding hands; nearness of heads on shoulders; caressing hair, arms, back and so on. It builds up sexual tension and arousal.

4. You should keep doing it during sex, not just before

Stretching out the sensuality is very erotic: No rushing from caressing to intercourse. Instead, foreplay is something to be lingered over. After all, it's often the longest part of the entire sexual encounter. Foreplay is all about seduction, conversation, touching the body. It's all that, and that should go on throughout lovemaking. Most people get lazy about it as a relationship progresses. Some tend to have a "Let's just get this orgasm" mentality. It's so shortened that it takes a lot of pleasure away.

5. Don't ignore other parts of the body during foreplay

All too frequently, people tend to go right for the erogenous zones when they're in bed. That's nice and all, but there are other parts of the body that shouldn't be overlooked during sex, and touching them helps build up excitement. The biggest mistake people make with women is to jump to the genitals right away and ignore the face, the neck, the earlobes, and just about anything else.

Men need to savor the whole body, rather than just try to get arousal through kissing and then move to intercourse. The abruptness of it makes it feel like the foreplay was just a con! Learn where your spouse's erotic zones are and target them.

6. Talk about what you want to get the most out of it

Communication is the key to good foreplay. Talk about what you want and need. Don't sit there and try to be polite in the moment. Have a sexy conversation with your spouse about what you like. And keep talking about it; one chat won't do it. It takes checking in over time. Just because something was effective as foreplay last night doesn't mean the same thing will work tonight. It's also important to give your partner feedback in the moment. During foreplay, it's good to make sounds and say, "This feels good," or "Oh I like that," etc. Giving some sort of confirmation or affirmation can take it to another level.

7. Foreplay isn't always what you'd expect

Think outside the box when it comes to what to do as foreplay. Even though most of us just focus on the "fooling around" part of it, there are other things that can serve as great foreplay too—whether it's massage, dirty dancing, wearing a sexy outfit, doing a little striptease, or just holding hands. Flirting is a form of foreplay. Women universally enjoy massages. Receiving a shoulder massage might be just the foreplay we need to relax into sex. Of course, other more obvious forms are almost always turn-ons for women too, especially oral sex (we're going to talk about that in a little more detail in a bit ☺). But don't forget about all those enticing little tidbits that can put you in the mood, too. Bottom line: Foreplay is just as important as sex itself, if not more so, especially for women. So, treat it that way! Most women need a lot of foreplay because we tend to be multi-taskers and are doing a lot of things, so getting into the mood for sex isn't as easy for us. When we're thinking about the kids and the laundry, it's good to have foreplay to get us slowly and gradually into the mood.

The Foreplay of Oral Sex

Is it right or not? Is this something we're supposed to do one to another and be okay with it? I've found over the years a lot of controversy in the Christian community as to whether or not this is okay. Many are confused about it. Many are totally okay with it, and then there are those who will say that it's not right and that it is completely against God's will.

So, let's talk about that for a minute. What is God's will in regards to oral sex for married couples? The Word always gives us the TRUTH that we need!

So, are there specific scriptures that actually discuss "oral sex"? The answer to that questions is "yes." Let's break this thing down:

Song of Songs chapters 4 and 5 New International Version (NIV)	Song of Songs chapters 4 & 5 The Message (MSG)
She	**The Woman**
[16] Awake, north wind,	[16] Wake up, North Wind,
and come, south wind!	get moving, South Wind!
Blow on my garden,	Breathe on my garden,
that its fragrance may spread everywhere.	fill the air with spice fragrance.
Let my beloved come into his garden	Oh, let my lover enter his garden!
and taste its choice fruits.	Yes, let him eat the fine, ripe fruits.
Chapter 5	**Chapter 5**
He	**The Man**
5 I have come into my garden, my sister, my bride;	5 I went to my garden, dear friend, best lover!
I have gathered my myrrh with my spice.	breathed the sweet fragrance.
I have eaten my honeycomb and my honey;	I ate the fruit and honey,
I have drunk my wine and my milk.	I drank the nectar and wine.
Friends	Celebrate with me, friends!
Eat, friends, and drink;	Raise your glasses—"To life! To love!"
drink your fill of love.	

Wow. Look at God! Even in scripture, He talks about how a man should partake of the woman's body! So, we see in Song of Songs (such a powerful love story) that the man makes reference to coming into the woman's garden. The woman's garden is his special place. This is the place where he breathes it in (smells of her goods). Not only does he breathe in her fragrance, but he also EATS whatever is in her garden! I love how it says, "I ate the fruit and the honey." Get it, Solomon! And he also states that he drinks the wine and the milk! Well, what is the wine or the milk? The wine/milk is the fluid that actually pours out of the woman's garden. Hmm…now I wonder what could that be? ☺ Solomon says that he drank it! Okay, so the Bible can get a little X-rated, but it's giving us the answers or the confirmations that we need, right? This clearly gives you the picture of oral sex being performed on a woman. It shows us how a man is supposed to enjoy every part of the woman's body by eating and drinking it all in! I love how he tells his friends to do the same and celebrate that they're doing it! Yessss!

We see how the Bible talks about the man eating the fruit of the woman, but what about the woman eating the fruit of the man?? Things that make you go….hmm! The question of the hour is….is it okay? Is it biblical for the woman to perform oral sex on her husband? And the answer is yes! Yes, yes and yes! According to the Word of God, it is most absolutely biblically correct to do this! Many people don't know that it's in the Bible. Allow me to break it down for you. We see that the man talks about oral sex with the woman in chapter 5 of Song of Songs. But check this out…before the man even talks about it with his wife, the woman is 3 chapters ahead of him doing it to him before he even does it to her! Wait…say what? Yes, it's true! Want to read all about it? Let me give it to you straight from the Word:

Song of Songs 2 New International Version (NIV)	Song of Songs 2 Amplified Version
She	*(The Shulammite Bride) Amplified*
[3] Like an apple[c] tree among the trees of the forest is my beloved among the young men. I delight to sit in his shade, and his fruit is sweet to my taste. [4] Let him lead me to the banquet hall,	3 "Like an apple tree [rare and welcome] among the trees of the forest, So is my beloved among the young men! In his shade I took great delight and sat down,

and let his banner over me be love. ⁵ Strengthen me with raisins, refresh me with apples, for I am faint with love. ⁶ His left arm is under my head, and his right arm embraces me.	And his fruit was sweet *and* delicious to my palate. "He has brought me to his banqueting place, And his banner over me is love [waving overhead to protect and comfort me]. 5 "Sustain me with raisin cakes, Refresh me with apples, Because I am sick with love. 6 "Let his left hand be under my head And his right hand embrace me."

Very interesting. So, let's break this down. She describes the man as like an "apple tree". She says that she wants to sit in his shade and eat. Think about this. To sit in the shade, he has to be standing over her. She desires to sit in his shade (with him standing over her) and eat "his fruit". She describes his fruit as "sweet and delicious" to her taste. So, as she is sitting in his shade eating, she says the banner that's over her signifies love. He loves her. She loves him, and that's why it's easy for her to eat his fruit. And get this. The Bible is so real. While she is eating "his fruit", his left hand is under her head and his right is embracing her while she's "eating". This gives a very vivid picture of what's going on here. Solomon wasn't playing, and she wasn't either!

So, as we can see, the Bible gives us a clear depiction of oral sex being performed on the man as well as on the woman. That's the answer to your question. Is it okay to perform oral sex on your spouse according to the Word of God? Absolutely! The Bible says that your body is not your own anymore when you're married. It's for your spouse to do what they want to do. Let me give you the scripture for that:

1 Corinthians 7 New International Version (NIV)	1 Corinthians 7 The Message (MSG)

7 Now for the matters you wrote about: "It is good for a man not to have sexual relations with a woman."[2] But since sexual immorality is occurring, each man should have sexual relations with his own wife, and each woman with her own husband. [3] The husband should fulfill his marital duty to his wife, and likewise the wife to her husband.[4] The wife does not have authority over her own body but yields it to her husband. In the same way, the husband does not have authority over his own body but yields it to his wife.[5] Do not deprive each other except perhaps by mutual consent and for a time, so that you may devote yourselves to prayer. Then come together again so that Satan will not tempt you because of your lack of self-control.

7 Now, getting down to the questions you asked in your letter to me. First, Is it a good thing to have sexual relations?

[2-6] Certainly—but only within a certain context. It's good for a man to have a wife, and for a woman to have a husband. Sexual drives are strong, but marriage is strong enough to contain them and provide for a balanced and fulfilling sexual life in a world of sexual disorder. The marriage bed must be a place of mutuality—the husband seeking to satisfy his wife, the wife seeking to satisfy her husband. Marriage is not a place to "stand up for your rights." Marriage is a decision to serve the other, whether in bed or out. Abstaining from sex is permissible for a period of time if you both agree to it, and if it's for the purposes of prayer and fasting— but only for such times. Then come back together again. Satan has an ingenious way of tempting us when we least expect it. I'm not, understand, commanding these periods of abstinence—only providing my best counsel if you should choose them.

In essence, your body belongs to your spouse. The husband can kiss and caress it any way that he desires. The same with the wife. It's perfectly okay. I will say this. If your spouse is not in a place of comfort when it comes to oral sex, then that has to be respected. If it's something that you feel like you must have, talk about it with your spouse. Get an understanding. Figure out ways that you can make it more comfortable or more desirable for them. I will even go so far as to say pray about it. The Bible says that we have not because we ask not. It's okay to ask God about your spouse desiring to have oral sex if it's something that's important to you. Whatever you do, don't hold back from having sex simply because you have an issue. The Bible says don't hold back unless you're doing it for fasting and praying purposes. Other than that, you and your spouse should be having sex often…in all kinds of ways and on all kinds of days! ☺ You abstain when you need to go to God about something. I know the women are like…okay, chill with that right now! We know that men can go all day every day if we let them. Here's the thing, though. Your husband desiring to be with you all the time is actually a good thing. We sometimes see it as a little frustrating. Not because of them, but because of the fact that we do so much throughout the day, sometimes sex can seem like another chore. Ladies, you have to change your mindset when it comes to this. You have to find a way to relax and enjoy the moment with your husband. You have to embrace all of his manhood. You have to give him the desires of his heart. Find a way to fulfill his needs even when you're tired, even when you've had a long day, even when you just don't feel like it. Marriage is about compromising, even when it comes to sex. You have to do what you have to do to keep your marriage healthy and whole, especially when it comes to sex. If you don't, another women will try to creep in and fill the void that you aren't filling. Leave NO room whatsoever for the enemy to come in! Do everything in your power to make sure that your marriage is whole, including having a healthy sex life!

Chapter 10

Let's TALK
Communication

Let's TALK Communication

I cannot stress how important it is to have communication in a marriage. Without communication, there's always an issue. With poor communication, there's always an issue. With little to no communication…guess what? There's going to be an ISSUE!

When you're not really talking to one another, it can cause bigger problems in your marriage. Marriage without communication, without exchange of thoughts, feelings, and emotions is unsustainable. You might find that you're not really mindful of making each other a priority, so when the communication starts to slip, the marriage can head into a danger zone. It doesn't mean that you can't fix it, but you want to be sure that you never take good communication for granted. There are some serious problems that can come about when the communication begins to suffer, and if you are aware of these and ensure that you keep things heading in the right direction, then love will conquer all.

Here are the reasons that a lack of communication in marriage can really be problematic:

1. You don't look to each other for support.

This might not sound like a big problem, but it really is. When you're married, you should be the first person that each of you turns to for support, help, and respect. When that is lacking, then you may turn to somebody else out of necessity, and this doesn't often end well. When you're not really talking or when you feel that you can't talk to each other, then the support goes away, and you become more like roommates.

How do you know if you're not being supportive of your spouse?

- You dismiss their concerns.
- You don't offer help when they are making decisions.
- You criticize them too much, too often, unnecessarily.
- You don't motivate them to achieve their dreams and aspirations.

When there is no communication in marriage between spouses, except for about things pertaining to your routines, understand there is inadequate support in your relationship. Remember that you should always lift each other up and talk to each other so the two are very closely linked. When you focus on good communication, then the support for each other comes much more naturally, so when you make these both a priority, you end up with a much happier marriage now and in the long term, too!

2. You may feel like you're living with a stranger.

If you've had a couple of days or weeks where you're not really talking, it can feel like you're living with a stranger. Though you may not mean for it to happen, lack of communication in a marriage can make you feel like you have lost each other. If this continues over time, then the intimacy eventually suffers, the connection is weakened and you find it hard to find common ground. Lack of communication in marriage leads to divorce sometimes when there is nothing left to share, when there is little to nothing to talk about between two partners.

Lack of communication in marriage leads to divorce. Beware of these signs that indicate that you and your spouse have become strangers.

- Your spouse is not able to read between the lines; he/she is unable to decipher your emotions.
- Your sex life dwindles. On top of that, other forms of physical connection like hugging and kissing become scarce.
- You have not dressed up and gone out for dates for a long time.
- Your communication is limited to discussing chores and finances.

You may find that you argue more and spend less and less time with one another. Though lack of communication or no communication on some days may not be a problem, if this continues over time, then you will have an undesirable situation and really crave that connection. Be aware of this and don't let conversations be on hold for too long if you want to stay connected and in love.

3. This can rob you of your connection over time.

You may wonder if it's normal or if a lack of communication in marriage is a problem. Think of this scenario playing out day after day for an extended period of time. When you're not talking, you may very well be turning to somebody else. You may lose the connection, the love, the passion, or the spark that you once shared.

Poor communication in marriage can make you tempted to cheat. It can make you feel like being married isn't quite what it used to be anymore. Everyone goes through rough times, but if you are aware of this and you make good communication a priority in your marriage, then you will stay connected and ensure that you don't head down the wrong path by losing each other.

Effects of lack of communication in marriage can be devastating to your relationship. It is important to identify and rectify all of your marriage communication problems before things fall apart between you and your spouse.

1) Take out 15 mins every day to talk about your day with your spouse.
2) Pay close attention to your spouse's body language. It will help you understand their mood.
3) Listen to your spouse attentively when he/she speaks. This will encourage them to have more conversations with you.

My husband and I have been married for decades now. When we first got married, we had to learn how to battle the communication beast. I was great at expressing my feelings, but my husband, on the other hand, wasn't so great at it. It was hard for him to express himself. His way of dealing with issues or concerns was to simply not say anything about it. He would just go with everything. It was hard for him to make decisions. It could be something as simple as figuring out where we were going to eat or what we were going to eat. It would always be my decision. That was soooo nerve wracking for me! Why couldn't he just open his mouth and say what he felt or say what he wanted? Why couldn't he just make a decision? Why was he such a "go with the flow" type of guy?

On one hand, I loved that he was so chill. On the other hand, I hated it. I needed him to express himself. I needed him to talk to me and tell me how he felt. I needed him to make decisions for our household. I knew that if we didn't figure this out soon, our marriage would be in trouble. Oh... did I mention that when we had an argument about something, instead of talking about issues, he would hardly say anything, and sometimes walk out when he was tired of hearing me go on and on? What? I thought that was the rudest thing! We had to figure that thing out and figure it out fast because I was not happy with the results that I was getting!

We both had a lot of learning and growing to do. Poor communication could have easily killed our marriage. He had to find his voice as a man, and I had to learn to balance my voice as a woman. It's easier said than done, especially when it's something that you're not used to doing. Nevertheless, we did what we had to do because one thing that we knew and we communicated well to one another was that we really wanted to be together. We didn't want to go anywhere. We wanted to be right where we were, which was together. I had to figure out how to let him be the man. I had to help him find his voice. I had to let him know that his voice mattered to me.

In helping my husband find his voice, there were things that I had to learn for myself. I want to share with the women 10 rules for promoting good communication with your husband. These certainly helped me, and I know they will help you as well.

Rule #1: There will be no non-subjects—period.

What is a non-subject? It's a subject that, for whatever reason, is understood to be off-limits and not to be brought up under any circumstance. Non-subjects between husbands and wives are not only sad, but destructive. They take away from the couple's chance for intimacy—for a heart-to-heart, soul-to-soul relationship. It takes two very mature people to handle painful subjects, but for the sake of a marriage, non-subjects must become discussable subjects. Patience is the key; don't give up until all subjects are open for discussion. This will help your marriage break barriers, knock down walls and kick the enemy out of your marriage!

Rule #2: Whatever you say, say it with love (Ephesians 4:15).

The more difficult something is to hear, the more gently and tenderly it must be said. Honesty without gentleness is brutal. Make sure that what you have to say needs to be said. Pray and ask God to give you wisdom about what to say and when to say it. Remember that men are really very vulnerable. Women are very emotional. Say it with love and sincerity—not with a "let me tell you something" attitude.

Rule #3: Timing is everything.

Don't try to talk about a difficult subject when the house is in chaos. Make a date. Go to a quiet restaurant and talk to him after he's had a good meal. Don't try to talk when he's getting ready to drift off to sleep. Set aside a special time that will allow you all to have great communication. Create an atmosphere of love and acceptance so that what is being said can be easily heard and received.

Rule #4: Get to the point.

We as women can go on and on…and on and on…and on and on! Don't say more than you have to. Give him the bottom line first; then go back and sketch in the details. He'll understand more of what you're saying. If he wants more information, he'll ask. One thing that men hate the most is when we as women babble about the same thing over and over and over again. Learn how to shorten your point and get to the bottom line of what you want, desire and need.

Rule #5: If he's not looking at you, he's probably not listening.

If you see his eyes drifting, it probably means you've said too much. He's lost interest. Get back to the point. Throw in a question. Give him room to say something. Make sure you're always in recognition of the atmosphere that he's giving you. Check his aura. Notice everything. Discern everything. Be alert. Know when he's gone from listening to not listening, attentive to not attentive, etc.

Rule #6: He can't read your mind.

If you're not willing to say it out loud, let it go. Don't expect him to pick up on your nonverbal hints. One of the biggest mistakes that we make about people is assuming they know. We make assumptions that simply aren't true, and when people fail at the assumptions that we've made, then we become upset at them for "not knowing, not doing, not being, etc." Assumptions can get you in a world of trouble. Assumptions can create a mess in your marriage. So stop assuming.

Rule #7: Be as positive as possible.

If you talk about problems all the time, he will tune you out. If you're positive most of the time, he'll be more willing to listen when you've got a problem Ephesians 4:29 says, *"Do not let any unwholesome talk come out of your mouths, but only what is helpful for building others up according to their needs, that it may benefit those who listen."* Ask God to give you better ways of addressing situations and issues with your spouse. When God gives you directions on how to do something, follow them.

Rule #8: Once you've shared your concerns, be quiet and listen.

Don't react; just listen. Your listening will let him know you are not attacking him and that you value his input. In James 1:19 we read, *"Dear friends, be quick to listen, slow to speak, and slow to get angry."* One of the things that I used to be really bad at was listening. I made it up in my mind that whenever my husband talked, I was going to hush my mouth and just listen. I wanted him to communicate, right? So why not give him a chance to say what he desires? After he does, then I respond; however, I make sure that I respond in love. Doing this has certainly taken the way we communicate to another level!

Rule #9: When the time comes, be willing to accept correction from your husband.

Don't be defensive. He must also be allowed to share concerns in a nonthreatening atmosphere. Be humble enough to let him lead you to a better place. Admit when he's right. Let him know that you will work on being better at what he's suggesting. You'll find that, in the end, it works. He'll love and respect you even more. Humility is the key.

Rule #10: Be forgiving.

Give your husband room to fail. Colossians 3:13 tells us to *"bear with each other and forgive whatever grievances you may have against one another. Forgive as the Lord forgave you."* It's a gift you give to one another. Bringing up old stuff will only take your marriage backwards. You will never progress that way. You have to get over the issues, no matter how hard or challenging they may be. Whatever happened, if you chose to love and forgive and move on, then that's exactly what you have to do. Don't renege on what you said you were going to do. The goal is to move forward. You must do exactly that, or your marriage will be completely destroyed. Don't let bitterness win. Let love win, and your marriage will prevail!

As you consider these rules, know that the bottom line is this: You have to work harder in having better communication between you and your spouse. Whatever level you're on right now, know that there is greater. There's another level after that. Every day and in every way, you want your marriage to continue to excel, especially when it comes to communicating. You never want to get to the point where you have "arrived". There's more. More FOR you and more FOR him. More FROM you and more FROM him. You simply have to be willing to give that "more". That's all.

Chapter 11

Forgiveness

Forgiveness

Being able to forgive and to let go of past hurts is a critical tool for a marriage relationship. Additionally, being able to forgive is a way to keep yourself healthy, both emotionally and physically. In fact, forgiving and letting go may be one of the most important ways to keep your marriage going strong.

If you hold on to old hurts, disappointments, petty annoyances, betrayals, insensitivity, and anger, you are wasting both your time and your energy. Nursing a perceived hurt can eventually turn it into something more—hatred and extreme bitterness.

Lack of forgiveness can wear you down. Additionally, being unforgiving is not good for either your physical or mental well-being. Resentment gains momentum and chips away at the foundation of your relationship. In the end, you'll find that holding things against your spouse will only hurt you and them. Holding pain is not worth the quality of your relationship. Holding bitterness is not worth hindering the quality of your life. The truth is you simply become UNHEALTHY—mentally, physically, emotionally, relationally, etc.

Here are few keys to forgiving your spouse:

- Be open and receptive to forgiveness.
- Make a conscious decision to forgive your spouse.
- When images of the betrayal or hurt flash in your mind, think of a calming place or do something to distract yourself from dwelling on those thoughts.
- Do not throw an error or mistake back in your spouse's face at a later date. Also, do not use it as ammunition in an argument.
- Do not seek revenge or retribution. Trying to get even will only extend the pain. Chances are, this won't really make you feel better anyway.
- Accept that you may never know the reason for the transgression, behavior or mistake.
- Remember that forgiveness does not mean you condone the hurtful behavior.
- Be patient with yourself. Being able to forgive your spouse takes time. Don't try to hurry the process.
- If you continue to be unable to forgive or you find yourself dwelling on the betrayal or hurt, please seek professional counseling to help you let go and forgive. In that moment,

you have to realize that you need help if you're really going to get past it. Be humble enough to admit that YOU NEED HELP.

On the other hand, if you are the one that committed the hurt or betrayal, I want to give you a strategy on how to ask for forgiveness when you have hurt your spouse:

- Show true contrition and remorse for the pain that you've caused.
- Be willing to make a commitment to NOT hurt your spouse again by repeating the same hurtful behavior.
- Accept the consequences of the action that created the hurt.
- Be open to making amends.
- Be patient with your spouse. Being able to forgive you often takes time. Don't dismiss your spouse's feelings of betrayal by telling your spouse to "get over it."
- Make a heartfelt and verbal apology. This includes a plan of action to make things right.

Marriage, like other close relationships, needs forgiveness to thrive. Remember that everyone makes mistakes. We all have bad or grumpy days. Many people say things they don't mean now and then. Everyone needs to forgive and to be forgiven. This is especially true if the person who hurt you is attempting to make amends and seek forgiveness. No relationship, especially a marriage relationship, can be sustained over a long period of time without forgiveness. Even though you may find it difficult to forgive, being able to do so is crucial in a marriage.

Now here is a major question that some people may have. Are some things unforgivable? The answer is no. All things are forgivable. You have to learn to love despite the hurt, pain, toil, and agony. Some things can lead to divorce, and that's fine if it's what GOD told you to do; however, in the midst of it all, you still have to find a way to forgive. Forgiveness is for you. Forgive and move on. Don't hang on to hurt and bitterness, no matter WHO gave you the reason to be broken. If your spouse abuses you, continues to betray you, keeps lying to you or makes no real change in behavior, then it may be time to say enough is enough, but you must always seek God for this truth. This calls for you to seriously evaluate your marriage and possibly think about divorce if there is continuous betrayal like adultery and even physical abuse. Be led by God as to what He desires for your life. God gives us grounds for divorce, but He definitely prefers reconciliation if it's possible. It can only be possible if both are willing to change their mindset and ways and come together on one accord in love, peace, and unity. When there is enough proof that these major concerns are not going away, despite your effort to forgive, your marriage is in trouble. You must seek godly help and professional help in extreme cases like this.

In some situations where there was an extended period of abuse or betrayals, but it is no longer occurring, forgiveness for the past hurts may take longer, and that is okay. You both must be open to talking about it and continuing to process it. It is encouraged to seek guidance from counselors and men and women of God that you can trust to help you through this.

Power of FORGIVENESS—Reasons to Forgive

There is a paradox behind forgiveness and the people we love the most. We know that those who are closest to us have the power to hurt us in great lengths, too. In these instances, it may be difficult to forgive your spouse.

When disappointments creep in, when arguments arise...what are you supposed to do? It may be human nature to distance yourself and give a cold shoulder to your spouse. However, these types of actions will not only cause more distance, they may also promote more misunderstandings in the future. This is why the Bible, the manual of life, highlights the importance of forgiveness.

Is it hard to forgive your spouse? Sometimes, yes. Is it impossible? No. You simply have to be willing to do it. There may be some things that he or she has done, such as had an affair, put you through some form of abuse, or constantly hurt you over the same things again and again. In these instances, I encourage you to go through counseling sessions. It may be in your best interest to go and get help, especially when you see that you can't do it alone. If forgiving your spouse seems impossible for you, that's a true sign to get someone else involved in helping you do it. It doesn't matter if you reconcile or not. If you have a hard time forgiving, then you MUST get someone to help you with that. Forgiveness is for YOU. Staying in an unforgiving place is NOT an option. Forgiveness is the key to your healing from whatever happened to you. You simply have to want to forgive. As husband and wife, here are some great reasons why you should learn to forgive your spouse on a day to day basis.

1. It creates the atmosphere for openness.

One of the great benefits of forgiving your partner is helping them feel more open with you. When there is tension in your relationship, it feels as though you are not free to express what you think and feel. When you learn to forgive, you put your defenses down, and your spouse does that too. It helps you become more open to talking about the problems or things that go through your mind.

2. It helps you develop affection for each other.

I'll give you a hypothetical situation. Suppose you had two bosses—one is cold and unforgiving and very strict about requirements. The other one is reasonable, warm, and forgiving. Who would you love more? The second boss, right?

The same goes for relationships. People develop affection for others who know how to be warm and forgiving. Tenderness goes a long way in your relationship. If you are always cold, strict and relentless in pointing out mistakes, your spouse may be discouraged to feel affection for you or to even be close to you. They'll always run from you until they can completely get away from you. Forgiving them helps you learn how to be affectionate again.

3. It also helps YOU become forgiven.

Another benefit that comes when you forgive your spouse is the chance to be forgiven. Your spouse is not perfect, and you aren't either. You cannot say that you haven't made mistakes in your relationship. There are ways that you may have hurt them that you may not even be aware of. Putting yourself in a position to forgive also helps others to forgive you. A seed of forgiveness will reap a harvest of you being forgiven. It's the law of attraction.

In Luke 6:37, Jesus tells us, *"Judge not, and you will not be judged; condemn not, and you will not be condemned; forgive, and you will be forgiven."* By forgiving your partner, you also have the opportunity to be forgiven. It isn't just about keeping score; it's about loving and understanding where your spouse is coming from.

Experience the blessings of an imperfect marriage. We all, at one time or another, have the opportunity to act right when our spouse acts wrong. There are no perfect marriages or perfect spouses. We know that having a good marriage requires effort and hard work, yet we often don't know how to continue to love when we are angry, hurt, scared, or just plain irritated. Nor are we sure what that kind of love is supposed to look like. Should we be patient? Forgive and forget? Do something else entirely?

Acting right when your spouse acts wrong will not necessarily guarantee a more satisfying marital relationship, nor will it automatically make your spouse change his or her ways, although both could occur. It will, however, help you see how God is stretching you in the midst of your marital difficulties, teaching you to respond wisely when wronged and leading you into a deeper relationship with Christ as you yield your will to His plan for your life and learn to be more like Him.

4. It renews and restores your relationship.

With forgiveness, there is a clean slate. There is a chance for your relationship to be renewed. When couples learn to forgive each other, they give each other a brand-new start to show their love.

5. Because God forgave...

The most important reason why you should forgive your spouse is understanding that God has already forgiven you. Ephesians 4:32 says, *"Be kind to one another, tenderhearted, forgiving one another, as God in Christ forgave you."* When we sinned, we were meant to deserve judgment for what we did. But God intervened, and we experienced forgiveness like no other. Wouldn't it be a way for us to glorify Him by extending the forgiveness that He gave to us? He modeled forgiveness so that we could learn to forgive others, too. Learn to forgive and repair your relationship. You'll feel better, not bitter, whole not broken when you do it.

Chapter 12

The P31 Woman...
Who is She??

The P31 Woman...Who is She??

Epilogue: The Wife of Noble Character

10 [b]*A wife of noble character who can find?*
She is worth far more than rubies.
11 *Her husband has full confidence in her*
and lacks nothing of value.
12 *She brings him good, not harm,*
all the days of her life.
13 *She selects wool and flax*
and works with eager hands.
14 *She is like the merchant ships,*
bringing her food from afar.
15 *She gets up while it is still night;*
she provides food for her family
and portions for her female servants.
16 *She considers a field and buys it;*
out of her earnings she plants a vineyard.
17 *She sets about her work vigorously;*
her arms are strong for her tasks.
18 *She sees that her trading is profitable,*
and her lamp does not go out at night.
19 *In her hand she holds the distaff*
and grasps the spindle with her fingers.
20 *She opens her arms to the poor*
and extends her hands to the needy.
21 *When it snows, she has no fear for her household;*
for all of them are clothed in scarlet.
22 *She makes coverings for her bed;*
she is clothed in fine linen and purple.
23 *Her husband is respected at the city gate,*
where he takes his seat among the elders of the land.

24 She makes linen garments and sells them,
and supplies the merchants with sashes.
25 She is clothed with strength and dignity;
she can laugh at the days to come.
26 She speaks with wisdom,
and faithful instruction is on her tongue.
27 She watches over the affairs of her household
and does not eat the bread of idleness.
28 Her children arise and call her blessed;
her husband also, and he praises her:
29 "Many women do noble things,
but you surpass them all."
30 Charm is deceptive, and beauty is fleeting;
but a woman who fears the LORD is to be praised.
31 Honor her for all that her hands have done,
and let her works bring her praise at the city gate.

Who exactly is this woman? If you're anything like me (and a lot of women I know), then the Proverbs 31 woman can be hard for you to understand sometimes. Sometimes we get mad at her. How can she be so perfect? How can we be expected to live that way? Is that really what Christian men are looking for in a wife? It seems so unattainable!

The Proverbs 31 woman did not do all of the things listed in this chapter in one day. She did them all throughout her lifetime. Proverbs 31 is NOT about a list of things we have to do every day. It's about an attitude. It's about doing things in excellence, taking care of your family and your household with a smile on your face. It's about making business transactions with wisdom and working diligently to chase your dreams. It's about knowing how to delegate, knowing how to put things in order; it's about developing a system that works for every aspect of your life so that your family, business, finances, ministry, etc. are all in order! And it's about giving God all the glory along the way.

Becoming a Proverbs 31 woman is no easy feat. In fact, if you jump in and start trying to be a virtuous wife and godly woman by using Proverbs 31 as a checklist, you'll end up defeated and exhausted from striving.

Any study of biblical womanhood is bound to land you in Proverbs 31 at some point. And if you're not careful, it will leave you feeling helpless, hopeless, overwhelmed, and downright frustrated.

In my studies, I found a few things about the Proverbs 31 woman that I want to share with you:

1. WHO IS THE PROVERBS 31 WOMAN?

The Proverbs 31 woman is one of the most misunderstood people in the Bible…because she isn't actually a person. When you do a Proverbs 31 Bible study, that's the first thing you need to know.

When you look to the *virtuous woman in the Bible* as your example, you're holding yourself up to an ideal—*not* a reality. And that's dangerous, because you will always fall short of an ideal. The first thing you need to know about her is that she isn't real; she is an ideal and included in scriptures to encourage and inspire us, but she wasn't a real woman doing all of those things all of the time.

> *The virtuous woman in the Bible isn't really a woman at all; she is intended to be a "type" for all godly women to follow…but not fall short of.*

2. WHAT WAS THE PROVERBS 31 WOMAN'S PURPOSE?

The Proverbs 31 woman was never meant to be *your* role model, but rather a story told to a son by a mother who wanted him to *appreciate* a godly wife. The purpose of Proverbs 31 was instructional. It was written as a poem so that it would be easy to remember, and it was intended to guide a king's choice in choosing a godly help. This is what this mother was teaching to her son. This is something that we need to teach to our young boys in order to encourage them to pursue a godly woman who is virtuous.

But we also need to teach them to love her with grace and not highlight her shortcomings. The Proverbs 31 woman describes a woman well-seasoned and experienced; a young wife would need to grow and experience years before being able to model all of the Proverbs 31 virtues.

In some families on Shabbat (Jewish holiday), the husband will read the passage in Proverbs 31 over his wife to honor and appreciate her. He will literally honor the bride of his youth as the virtuous woman in the Bible. How beautiful!

The second thing to remember about the Proverbs 31 woman is that she was created by a mother (inspired by God) to instruct her son in how to choose a godly wife. As moms, we need to remember this and teach our sons about the women they will someday marry—both how to choose them and how to honor them.

The virtuous woman in the Bible is a model to hold before our sons, to teach them what to pray for, look for, and celebrate when they find her.

3. WHAT HABITS DOES A PROVERBS 31 WOMAN HAVE?

A look at the Proverbs 31 woman's ministry is truly daunting if you feel like you have to measure up to this Biblical standard right now. But a grace-filled Proverbs 31 Bible study makes it clear that she was a seasoned wife who had spent years cultivating her own life and heart.

She was a blessing to her husband and children, respected in the city, and well thought of by those she did business with. While it might be easy to infer that she was a business-savvy entrepreneur (which she certainly was!), it's more important to realize *that long before she tended vineyards, she tended herself.* She applied Biblical principles in her marriage, motherhood, and ministry, and that is what led to such fruitful results.

The third thing to remember about the Proverbs 31 woman when you read through this scripture is that while her appearance is never mentioned, her godly heart is. The Wise Mama told her son to look for what really matters in a wife and to appreciate the things of eternal value.

The virtuous woman in the Bible was one who knew where true value was and invested in that.

As women, we should take our cues from this and spend more time in prayer than on primping and more time cultivating our character than our wardrobe. It's time to tend the habits that feed our soul and bless God and our families more than anything else.

4. WHAT IS A PROVERBS 31 WOMEN'S MINISTRY?

What exactly is a Proverbs 31 ministry anyhow? I've heard so many women over the years refer to different projects as their Proverbs 31 women's ministry. I suppose it makes us feel better when we can slap a label on our homemaking that makes it sound sweeter. But why do we need one? The ministry of the Proverbs 31 woman wasn't buying and selling fields or trading with merchants or selling her wares. It wasn't helping her husband's career. It was honoring God.

The fourth thing you need to know about the Proverbs 31 woman is that her ministry wasn't about her accomplishments at all; it was about eternity. Her virtues, her business, and her awesome talents were simply fruit of a heart that honored God and ministered in the ways that He directed.

The virtuous woman in the Bible prized relationship over accomplishment. She lived a "Martha life" with a "Mary heart".

You can't go wrong when you love God and obey Him. Don't let anything else distract you and keep you so busy that you forget what matters most.

5. WHAT IS THE PROVERBS 31 WOMAN ALL ABOUT?

So many times, we look at where we want to be in life and lament that we aren't there *right now*. But the Proverbs 31 woman is all about *becoming*.

It takes time to mature in the Lord and cultivate those virtues in your life.

The truth is that it's about embracing God's grace, bearing God's image, and fulfilling God's call on your life. The Proverbs 31 woman exudes Jesus brightly.

It's about becoming more like Jesus. It's not focusing on virtues or skills or activities.

If you remember nothing else about her, remember that the virtuous woman in the Bible is a beautiful example of what we ought to become: a Jesus-reflecting, image-bearing, fruitful woman of God.

THE NEXT PROVERBS 31 WOMAN: YOU

So, are you up for it? Are you ready to be a modern-day virtuous woman? Are you ready to join the ranks of the Proverbs 31 woman army? It's comprised of women just like you who love God and their families. It's made up of women who love the Lord with all their hearts, souls, minds, and strength and long to make God happy with their faith. It's an army that will change the world, one marriage and one generation at a time. And you are a Proverbs 31 woman when you cultivate your heart with the Word and prayer and live a life that bears the fruit of the Scriptures and love. You can be the virtuous woman in the Bible *today.*

Let's go back and look at the scriptures and break down the virtues that the P31 woman possessed. Let's start with verse 10:

10- VIRTUE

The first line begins by telling women they are precious and worthwhile. God calls us to be virtuous and capable. I truly believe that a P31 woman knows and understands her worth. To be the P31 woman, you have to be confident about who you are to God and to the world that He put you in.

11- FAITHFULNESS

We are called to speak the truth and to earn the trust of others. We are to be faithful and to enrich not only our lives, but the people around us as well. We are to show faithfulness to our husbands, faithfulness to our kids, and faithfulness to everything that God has given and called us to. We have to show God, ourselves, and others around us that we can be trusted with that which has been given to us.

12- GOODNESS

We are called to be good to our husbands and family, to cherish them and love them. Goodness is all about moral excellence, virtue, kindness, and generosity. Displaying goodness to others brings about blessings and prosperity to our own lives.

13- HARDWORKING

God calls us to be hard workers, never lazy, and always improving ourselves. The P31 woman will work hard on her marriage, her job, and her business, taking care of the kids, and keeping her finances in order. She's always ahead of the game, ready to do what is necessary to keep her life in order…even when she's tired.

14- PROVIDER

This verse talks about providing the family with food, cooking, and serving. This can be taken literally, or as I see it, to care for and help your family. She will make sure that the house is in order. She will take what she has, and use it, whether it's a lot or if it's a little. It will work because the P31 woman knows how to make it work!

15- EARLY RISER

God calls us to wake up before dawn (maybe one of the hardest tasks for me as I am truly NOT a morning person) and prepare for the day. I see this as God calling us to be hardworking and purposeful with our time. I start my day in prayer and then prepare for the day. The P31 woman does not sleep and slumber away the day. She gets up, ready to make it happen, ready to do what she has to do. She's ready to get up and make her day great…on purpose and with purpose!

16- BUSINESS SAVVY

This verse was one I had a hard time with. Many people read the Bible and think women should stay home and be housewives. While there is nothing wrong with that, the Lord also calls on us to work hard, earn an income, and help our family. It is our job to pay attention to our world and take advantage of opportunities. Mind you, I am not saying that every woman should start a business. Everyone is NOT called to be a business owner. If that were the case, who would be left to work it, to help run it, or to help it grow? A P31 woman knows how to handle business, whether it be for her job or for her very own business. She will do things in excellence. Being lazy is NOT an option!

17- STRENGTH

Energetic and Strong. This can be your physical strength (working out, health, etc.), mental strength (being there for others when they need help), or spiritual strength (asking God for guidance and praying). We are called to do these things with optimism and energy. And when you feel yourself getting weary and tired, do what Nehemiah did in the Bible. He asked God to strengthen his hands so that he could do the work that God had called him to do. Don't be afraid to ask God the same thing when you feel yourself getting burned out, tired, and ready to forget everything and everybody. Remember, quitting is NOT an option. A P31 woman has to continue to move forward in purpose!

18- ENDURANCE

Again, we are called to be hard workers. Not only that, but God asks us to ensure that our dealings are well handled, even if it means staying up late. We are called to endure during hard times and to continue to work hard until we see the manifestation of whatever it is that we are believing God for. We have to endure until the end.

19- WELL-ROUNDED

This verse was another hard one for me. I decided that because verse 13 talks about wool and flax, this comparison calls for us to be well-rounded and understanding of many skills. God calls us to learn and grow, and by learning different skills, we can help our family. Never stop learning. Never stop growing. Never stop developing yourself into being ALL that God has called you to be!

20- CHARITABLE

We are called to help the poor and less fortunate. We are told to love our neighbors, and this verse calls us to love those in need by welcoming them with open arms. We should show love to every man, according to the Word of God. Showing love to people daily is a dynamic virtue of the P31 woman.

21- PROVIDE AND TRUST

This verse has two key ideas, one being that it is our job to provide for our kids and family, to keep them safe and loved. The second is trusting in God and His plan. Even during hard times, trusting in our work and His is key. No matter what it looks like, the P31 woman knows how to trust God. She knows to have hope in the Lord, that He has already brought provision, and because of that, the P31 woman chooses to walk by faith in the belief that things are already done, and her house is already provided for by the Almighty God!

22- WELL-DRESSED

Being a fashionista and a women's boutique owner, I LOVE THIS ONE! This verse is interesting. God asks us to not be consumed by our looks, but here He tells us to be well-dressed. The idea is to treat ourselves like we are worth it, which we are! As women, we have to make sure to keep ourselves together. We can't walk around looking like we have been working all day, and we're just TIRED! No, ladies! We have to get up and be FABULOUS in every way, including our looks! Get your hair done, wear nice clothes (a little makeup won't hurt), smell good, look good...FEEL GOOD! The description of this woman is not of a woman who walks around in sweats and a T-shirt all day. Step it up! Whatever level you're on right now, there's always a NEXT level! It's time that we started acting like it!

23- WIFE TO A GOOD HUSBAND

This verse is God telling us to marry a man who is a good husband and a good leader. There are many places that talk about marriage in the Bible. I think this verse reiterates that God calls us to marry a man with the same faith as ourselves. That's called being "equally yoked". Someone who loves God will be a good husband and leader. I didn't say perfect, but he will be good. A marriage that is centered around the things of God and not selfish gain or selfish ambitions will always work out, no matter what you're going through. You have to make sure you marry well so that the marriage will work out for your good! There are so many godly women out there right now who are struggling still today after many years of marriage simply because they didn't marry a man of God. They were hoping and wishing that he would change, and to this day...still no change. I'm not saying that it's impossible; I'm just saying that the struggle is more real when you become unequally yoked with someone spiritually.

24- WORKING

Here's another verse calling us to work for an income. God wants us to provide for ourselves and family. He asks us to sell our work and earn a living. It's okay for women to work and help take care of the home. After all, we are called "helpmates." I know that in some cultures, it is like a sin to do this; however, in our culture, it's totally cool for a woman to work, start a business, be CEO, CFO, etc. If God put in you a hope, wish, or dream to do something in the workforce, then do it as unto the Lord! It will work if you work!

25- HONORABLE

This is one of my favorite verses. We are called to fear nothing but God. We are told to be honorable and strong and to carry ourselves as graceful women. We are also told to laugh, to be happy and optimistic. When you carry yourself with grace, class, and style, people will look at you and call you blessed. Your children will rise up and call you blessed. You will win the favor of many, and the honor of God will rest upon your life. You are an honorable P31 woman!

26- WISE

We are asked to think before we speak and to always do so with kindness. It is asked that we be wise with what we say. For many women, this is so hard to do! Why is it that we as women ALWAYS have something to say? We are very opinionated. We are very expressive! But God wants us to be quick to listen and slow to speak. We have to watch our attitudes. We have to send out seasoned words of wisdom. We have to be willing to show love and compassion. A P31 woman is as wise as a serpent but as gentle as a dove!

27- ACTIVE

Laziness is not an option. God calls us to take care of our homes (and families) and to work hard for them. Not only that, but we also need to take care of our bodies, our souls, our minds, and our peace. We have to take care of every aspect of our lives so that we can walk in the fullness of what God has for us. That means work out. Eat healthy. Pray and fast. Seek quiet moments of peace. Do whatever is needed to ensure that you are actively living the life that God has called you to live!

28- PRAISE-WORTHY

We are promised thanks and praise for our hard work. We are asked to take these praises and give back to our families. Our children will call us blessed. Our husbands shall honor and adore us. We shall have favor with man and favor with God. The P31 woman is worthy of praise! You are worthy of praise! Never doubt that!

29- EXCELS

With God in our hearts, we can achieve anything we set our sights on. We are told that we will succeed and excel. We simply have to trust God and trust the process that He has us on.

30- GOD-FEARING

We are called to fear the Lord. He is the only One that we should fear, and through that fear, we will come to know Him and accept Him into our hearts. We are told to live in a way that honors God.

31- REWARDED

The last verse tells us that we will be praised for our hard work and dedication. God promises to recognize our faith. Faith in God and what He has given us always brings about blessings, increase, favor, abundance, and wealth. Prosperity is our portion when obedience is submitted unto God. God will cause us to be a prosperous people in Him!

HOW TO APPLY PROVERBS 31 TO YOUR LIFE

Obviously, that is a lot to take in. We are not perfect, nor does God expect us to be. Becoming a Proverbs 31 woman means working hard to become a woman who honors God, even when it comes to taking care of her home. To simplify this even more, I have a list of things I try to do daily/weekly/monthly that help me become closer to God:

- Remember that you are worthy of God's grace.
- Be truthful and faithful.
- Love others, be good to others, and pray for others.
- Work hard in everything you do.
- Wake up early and start the day with God. Pray every day and praise our Lord.
- Study and learn. Enrich your life with knowledge and understanding, and become well-rounded in your skills.
- Take advantage of opportunities in business, helping others, and caring for others.
- Be strong and endure hard times. Put your faith in God to help you when you feel lost.
- Love and honor yourself; dress well, exercise, and behave well. Take care of the temple that God has blessed you with.

- If you're not married yet, make sure you marry a husband who shares your values and love for God.
- Fear God and honor Him in all things.
- Remember that you are praise-worthy and will be rewarded for your work.

Here are some steps to becoming and remaining the P31 woman that God desires for you to be:

1. **Make your spouse's life better than it was before.** Proverbs 31:10-12 says, *"A wife of noble character who can find? She is worth far more than rubies. Her husband has full confidence in her, and lacks nothing of value. She brings him good, not harm, all the days of her life."*

   - It is interesting that it says, "A wife of noble character who can find?", meaning that it is a very rare thing. But if you are such a wife, you are worth far more than rubies! That is an incentive to become a wife of rare quality, right? If you are worth far more than rubies, then you are highly prized. That is always a good thing when it comes to marriage.
   - Why does her spouse have confidence in her? Because she causes good, not harm; she is a good person. Her spouse knows that she won't cheat or abandon the family because she has integrity. She will work hard, show her love, and talk about problems when they arise instead of hiding them.
   - Contrast this with another verse in Proverbs, *"[It is] better to live on a corner of the roof than share a house with a quarrelsome wife"* *(Proverbs 21:9).* Don't pick fights. Bring up problems respectfully, without taking out your frustrations on your spouse. Obviously, if you try to fight with your partner all the time, that would cause harm and not good. So, seek to address problems respectfully and constructively.

2. **Take good care of your family.** Proverbs 31:13-15 says, *"She selects wool and flax and works with eager hands. She is like the merchant ships, bringing her food from afar. She gets up while it is still night; she provides food for her family and portions for her female servants."*

   - The modern equivalent would mean working hard on whatever your job for the family is. Depending on the division of labor in your family, you may have a career and/or chores at home. Stay on top of your responsibilities. Don't let work pile up. Ask for help if you need it.

- It is interesting that it says, *"She gets up while it is still night."* This is a reality for any mother with small children already, but the idea is to selflessly help your family as much as you can. Do what you can to meet the needs of your family, especially any children who can't care for themselves yet. Of course, you still need to make sure you're getting enough rest; you're not helpful to anyone if you're physically or emotionally exhausted.
- Talk to your spouse about what to do if you feel overwhelmed by your responsibilities. You may need to reallocate the work or even hire someone to help with cooking and cleaning. Problem-solve together about how you can ensure that the work gets done without exhausting anyone.

3. **Be wise with your money.** Proverbs 31:16 says, *"She considers a field and buys it; out of her earnings she plants a vineyard".* Make great decisions when it comes to what you purchase. In our modern day, don't get fooled by advertisers who want to sell you anything and everything. *Consider* what you buy before you buy it, in everything. Be a good steward with your money and what you choose to buy.

- You may not literally plant a vineyard, but you can make money in other ways. Write, make jewelry, tutor, or find another way to make extra money if you can. You can also learn about the stock market and buy some index funds for long-term gain. Learn about investments. Get a strategy for another source of income. Everyone is not called to be a business owner. That's not what I'm saying. I'm saying that you can use wisdom in how to bring more money into your home and your bank accounts.
- There is a comical quote that says, *"Lucky is the man who can make more than his wife spends."* But seriously, don't overspend. Divorce is often caused by arguments over money. Issues with finances is one of the top three reasons people are getting divorces today. Think before you spend. Big purchases should only be made if both spouses agree.
- Verse 27 says she *"does not eat the bread of idleness."* Don't waste your time and be idle doing nothing. There are plenty of jobs that you can do from home if

you're a stay-at-home mom, such as telemarketing, sewing, writing, graphic design, etc. You could even make a little extra income by selling items that you no longer need or want (like toys your kids have outgrown, books and DVDs you've already read, electronics you've replaced, etc.) on eBay. Try to make good use of your time and be productive.

4. **Be a hard worker.** Proverbs 31:17 says, *"She sets about her work vigorously; her arms are strong for her tasks"*. Find things to do to help your family. The Bible says, *"Whatever you do, work at it with all your heart, as working for the Lord, not for human master" (Colossians 3:23).* You are working to serve your spouse and children, but primarily you are working to serve God. You may think at times that your family doesn't deserve your hard work, but you are not working for them, per se; you are working for God. Serve God by serving the needy and your family and children, teaching them to serve others.

Some say that motherhood is the most thankless job because you never get a promotion or public recognition. You just do all of your tasks humbly and quietly. This is why some women get frustrated about the work they have to do. Always remember, you are working as unto God. God will reward you for what you do. Don't worry. Jesus said in Matthew 6:19-20, *"Do not store up for yourselves treasures on earth, where moths and vermin destroy, and where thieves break in and steal. But store up for yourselves treasures in heaven, where moths and vermin do not destroy, and where thieves do not break in and steal."* There may not be many rewards in this life, but you are building treasures in heaven with everything you do for your family.

1 Cor. 3:14-15 says, *"If what has been built survives, the builder will receive a reward. If it is burned up, the builder will suffer loss but yet will be saved—even though only as one escaping through the flames."* Whatever we build on the foundation of Jesus in our lives is what we will be rewarded for in heaven, even if it doesn't last. Every selfless deed, every act of love, we will be rewarded for in heaven someday. Of course, knowing that God will reward you doesn't mean you should suffer in silence. It's okay to say, "Sometimes I feel unappreciated" or "I get overwhelmed at times, and I need more help around the house." Be assertive, even if things aren't going well.

5. **Be a generous and kind person.** Proverbs 31:20 says, *"She opens her arms to the poor and extends her hands to the needy."* Find ways to help others in your everyday life. Do it regardless of whether other people can see.

- Donate money or old clothes to charity.
- Try volunteering at a food kitchen, tutoring center for disadvantaged students, homeless shelter, animal shelter, hospital, or other places dedicated to helping people in need.
- Avoid judging people who are in bad situations, even if they made mistakes. Instead, ask them how you can help.
- Vote mindfully. Never vote for politicians who would disenfranchise the oppressed.

6. **Dress well without worrying too much about it.** Verse 22 does say, *"She is clothed in fine linen and purple."* So, this Proverbs 31 woman is well-dressed, but keep in mind verse 30: *"Charm is deceptive, and beauty is fleeting; but a woman who fears the Lord is to be praised."* The most important thing to keep attractive is your heart. Beauty is fleeting. Everyone ages, but you will have your heart and your character as long as you are alive. Work on cultivating your inner beauty more than your physical beauty.

7. **Speak respectfully of your spouse.** Verse 23 says, *"Her husband is respected at the city gate, where he takes his seat among the elders of the land."* Don't gossip about your spouse and insult his character. Speak in such a way about him to others so that others will respect him, including your kids.

- Know the difference between gossiping and asking for advice. Criticizing your spouse is bad. Confidentially asking for help solving a marital issue can be all right. There is a big difference between saying, *"My husband is so selfish,"* and *"How do I approach my husband about my frustration with this issue?"*
- Of course, this does not apply if you have an abusive spouse. Do not sugar-coat the truth to protect the reputation of a cruel man. Tell other people what is happening, and ask them to help you. Your safety and the safety of your children (if you have any) come first.

8. **Be a confident woman.** Verse 25 says, *"She is clothed with strength and dignity; she can laugh at the days to come."* Believe in your own strength and abilities. Trust that God has

your future in the palm of His hand. Then you can "laugh at the days to come". Be a woman of faith, not fear.

9. **Be wise and give advice where needed.** Verse 26 says, *"She speaks with wisdom, and faithful instruction is on her tongue."* In order to teach your children, seek to grow in wisdom. Read books. Listen to sermons. Read the Bible as much as you can. Pray for wisdom. When someone is upset, validate their feelings and listen closely to their sorrows. This can make them feel much better.

10. **Expect respect from your children and spouse.** Verses 28 and 29 say, *"Her children arise and call her blessed; her husband also, and he praises her: 'Many women do noble things, but you surpass them all.'"* Treat your family with respect, and expect them to do the same to you. Each one of you was created by God, and each one of you deserves to be treated with basic dignity. People tend to show respect for those who show respect for them. Treat your family respectfully, without losing control of your temper or calling names. (Take a break if necessary.) Avoid harsh punishments, and discipline fairly and compassionately.

11. **Do not take on more than you can handle.** Although God will help you, God helps those who help themselves. If you take on what you know you can't handle, God may not help you with that. Discuss how you feel. It's okay to say, "I'm overwhelmed," or "I've taken on more than I can handle." Reach out to others for assistance and advice.

In summary, being a P31 woman is a beautiful yet challenging calling. A P31 woman is one who is ever-evolving and ever-becoming. She stays consistent, even during hard times. She finds ways to make things happen for her home. She's loving and kind. She trusts the Lord. She does things as unto Him. She finds favor with God and favor with man. She chooses not to lean to her own understanding, but turns to the one that can direct her. She's beautiful. She's strong. She's YOU. Each and every day, strive to become better, wiser, smarter, and stronger. You'll then see yourself manifesting the wonderful attributes that the Proverbs 31 woman embodies. Remember that.

Chapter 13

The Final Judgment (From the Spouse, Derrick Morrissette)

The Final Judgment
(From the Spouse, Derrick Morrissette)

We often hear Proverbs 31 quoted to reference the ideal/model wife or woman. Proverbs 31 is the 31st Book of Proverbs in the Old Testament of the Christian Bible and is presented as advice which Lemuel's (a biblical King) mother gave to him, detailing the attributes of a virtuous wife or ideal woman. This chapter of Proverbs 31 has often been used as the standard of what a woman should be, or should I say what would make "The Fabulous Wife". The intent of Proverbs 31 is to show a young man the qualities he should look for in a wife and the things he should value in the fabulous wife. I must say Proverbs 31 is not an exhaustive list of what the fabulous wife is, but it is a good start on what the fabulous wife looks like. So, in retrospect, "The Proverbs 31 Woman" is not an actual person, but rather what the ideal, fabulous wife or ideal woman would look like. As you continue to read, I want to point out some of the attributes as it relates to *The Fabulous Wife*.

I want to talk about five attributes or qualities that I believe help make "The Fabulous Wife" that Proverbs 31 describes. I will make a disclaimer that this is not an exhaustive list or the be-all and end-all, but simply a set of characteristics and qualities to look for in The Fabulous Wife. Just think, if it was good for a wise mother to tell her son who was a king what to look for in a woman, it's probably good for any man. A godly wife should be virtuous, faithful, hardworking, wise, and have a good reputation.

Virtuous

*"Who can find a virtuous woman and
capable wife?*

She is more precious than rubies."

—Proverbs 31:10 (NLT)

One of the most important characteristics that should be exemplified by The Fabulous Wife is that she should be virtuous. Virtuous is defined as *having or showing high moral standards: ethical, lawful, honest, honorable, upright, not perfect but strives to walk in excellence.* A woman or person of virtue isn't perfect, but the Fabulous Wife or virtuous woman holds herself to high ethical standards. The Fabulous Wife is honest and honorable and is neither manipulative nor deceitful. When The Fabulous Wife operates in this manner, her reputation goes before her, and she exemplifies Proverbs 31:10. A woman of virtue is beautiful because that characteristic from within shows on the outside. Her virtue is seen in how she treats others and in all of her dealings in the marketplace and with her family.

A woman of virtue is hard to find, according to Proverbs 31:10, but when you do, the virtuous characteristics cause her to be even more valuable to all those she encounters. Proverbs 31:10 uses the analogy that a woman of virtue is more precious than rubies, diamonds, and gold. Some translations compare her wealth to be more precious than jewels. Jewels are truly a rare commodity. You have to search and mine diligently for them, but when you find them, you have a priceless treasure. Gold, diamonds, and rubies are valuable materials also and one of the most important features of them is that they hold their value and don't decrease over time. If you melt gold down, it still holds a value that can make one wealthy.

I know I'm not the only man who has a wife who embodies the characteristic of being virtuous, but I do want to use her as an example of the virtuous woman. She treats people with honor and also is an honorable person. She treats everyone as though they are special and are significant. She finds value in other people, so it makes it easy to honor them. One of my favorite quotes that speaks of humility is, "When dealing with people, you should treat the janitor the same way you would treat the CEO." That's the mindset that my Fabulous Wife lives by. Most of all, the way she carries herself makes her a virtuous woman. She walks upright, carrying herself in a very respectable way that commands respect when she enters an environment. She also holds true to her ethics, not lowering them to the world's standards. My wife exemplifies the characteristics of being virtuous, which helps her own the status of "The Fabulous Wife"!

Faithful

"Her husband can trust her, and she will greatly enrich his life. She brings him good, not harm, all the days of her life"
Proverbs 31:11-12 (NLT).

The second characteristic exemplified by The Fabulous Wife is faithfulness. Faithful is defined as *being firm in commitment to promises or duties*. Faithful carries the connotation of one who is loyal, unyielding, constant, steadfast, and who has a firm resistance. The characteristic of faithful in Proverbs 31:11 causes the man or husband to trust her with all that is within him with no reason to regret it, doubt it, or second-guess it. In other words, the man is saying "because of your consistent behaviors and your unwavering adherence to your promises and duties, I have no reason to think you will do anything outside of what you have been doing."

She has created a habit of being in harmony with her words and actions, which creates a habit of faithfulness. So, faithfulness is not only what she does, but who she is.

I once heard someone say that unfaithful people don't surprise them anymore, but faithful people do. I say that this is very unfortunate that one could have such a testimony. Proverbs 18:22 says, *"He who finds a wife finds a good thing and obtains favor from the Lord."* I also say, *"He that finds a faithful wife also is favored."* When a husband has found a faithful wife, he can be in a place of peace, knowing that she has his best interest and will not intentionally do things that will bring about hurt or harm to him.

I want to close on this characteristic of a faithful wife with an example of my faithful wife. There's a popular saying, "ride or die," which originally was a biker term, meaning if you couldn't ride, you would rather die. That means that you would stick closer than close to something you loved, or you would not part with something/someone you loved, no matter what. You were faithful and committed to that thing or person. It has changed to mean that you will "ride" any problems out with them or "die" trying…with them. She is faithful.

I myself have found this quality in my faithful wife and partner for life. We have had ups and downs, good times, and opportunistic times, tough and tougher times, but through it all, she has exemplified faithfulness—not only to me, but also to her vows. I believe most of all, one has to be faithful to oneself. If you do that, it will be easier to be faithful to others. I have found a faithful wife that Proverbs 31:11-12 speaks of, and she is more precious than rubies. She's not perfect, but she is FAITHFUL.

Hardworking

"She finds wool and flax and busily spins it. She is like a merchant's ship, bringing her food from afar. She gets up before dawn to prepare breakfast for her household and the day's work for her servant girls. She goes to inspect a field and buys it; with her earnings she plants a vineyard. She is energetic and strong, a hard worker. She makes sure her dealings are profitable; her lamp burns late into the night. Her hands are busy spinning thread, her finger twisting fiber" Proverbs 31:13-19 (NLT).

The third characteristic that's exemplified by The Fabulous Wife is being hardworking. She is hardworking and business savvy. The word "hardworking" is defined as *tending to work with energy and commitment, diligent and industrious*. She is also business savvy, meaning she has a quickness in understanding and dealing with business situations in a manner that is likely to lead to a good outcome. She is an expert in her field which comes together by a few traits that stand out. The hardworking and business savvy wife possesses the following skills: she's a "big picture" thinker; she has the ability to see how the key drivers of her business, family, etc., relate to each other; she uses knowledge to make good decisions and is not always emotionally driven; she understands how actions and decisions impact her surroundings, and she is an effective communicator.

I want to clarify that a hardworking wife isn't one who is always out in the marketplace or running a Fortune 500 organization with a healthy salary. A hardworking wife could certainly be one that is a stay-at-home mom who takes care of the children, making sure that the home is decent and orderly, and making sure her husband's and children's physical well-being is being taken care of. She uses her hands industriously. The word "industrious" means *one is constantly, regularly, or habitually active or occupied not working in an industry.* In Proverbs 31:13-19, the overall takeaway for "The Fabulous Wife" is she is constantly active in making sure her family, home, and activities are taken care of.

I have personally seen my wife do both. She has worked in the marketplace and has been a stay-at-home mother and wife, and has excelled at both. In both situations, she was diligent in hard work, working relentlessly with her hands, and bringing value and resources to our home. As a stay-at-home mother, she faithfully took care of our children, meeting all of my needs as a husband, all while building multiple businesses. She rose early in the morning while keeping the lamp on long into the night. She was industrious and is now a savvy business woman and is like a merchant ship, bringing goods from afar daily. She is "The Fabulous Wife".

Wise

"When she speaks, her words are wise and she gives instructions with kindness. She carefully watches everything in her household and suffers nothing from laziness."

The fourth absolutely important characteristic that must be exemplified by "The Fabulous Wife" is being wise. I emphasize this one with the utmost importance because I believe women were created to help the man and assist with carrying out God's plan. In doing so, not only must a man walk in wisdom, but the woman also. When one is not walking in wisdom, the other may be won over by the wisdom and behavior of the spouse. The word "wise" simply means *exercising or showing sound judgement*. It also means *to know the difference between right and wrong and behaving accordingly*. The Bible says, *"Wisdom is more precious than rubies and nothing you desire can compare with her"* (Proverbs 8:11). That's a strong statement that means you can have all things, but nothing you will ever have can compare to or is more important than having wisdom or being wise. You can have "the things", but it's wisdom that allows you to maintain them.

"The Fabulous Wife" is wise in her words, meaning she will think before she speaks and will examine her words before they flow out of her heart. That's right…out of her heart. When a person speaks, it's normally because it's something that's on the inside of them that comes out when the ideal situation presents itself. I believe this is equally important for men as well, to be fair. Men should also speak wisely and choose their words wisely. Our speech should be that which builds people up and not tears them down. The power of life and death are in your words, and "The Fabulous Wife" can use her words to build her husband up.

My wife and I have both had to grow in wisdom, and we continue to do so daily. As a man and husband, I have had to constantly refine my thoughts and actions to become wiser.

As I have done throughout this chapter, I want to give a practical example of wisdom in The Fabulous Wife. I can remember back when my wife and I were dating. She was the only female in a family of six siblings. Because of her being older than some of her brothers, she took on more responsibilities while her mom and dad worked by taking care of her younger brothers. As she learned right from wrong, she would often try and communicate that to her brothers, but the presentation and choice of words were a bit harsh. The conversations often didn't go well but always ended up with altercations and shouting back and forth. She was saying the correct things, but how she was saying them was not with the best presentation. But as she matured, she learned how to speak to them in a way that they could receive it. That's what wisdom does. She was able to apply knowledge by using wisdom in how to say it. My wife, The Fabulous Wife, is now able to better communicate with me and others. Because she took care of her brothers at a young age, she was able to transition those skills over to our home as a hard worker, and she is very watchful of things not being in order and not being excellent. She is The Fabulous Wife.

Good Reputation

"Her children arise and call her blessed; Her husband also, and he praises her: 'Many women do noble things, but you Surpass them all.' Charm is deceptive, and beauty is fleeing; but a woman who fears the Lord is to be praised. Honor her for all that her hands have done, and let her works bring her praise at the city gate."

The last and final characteristic that describes The Fabulous Wife is a good reputation. *Reputation is the belief or opinion that one believes about another person or thing.* Reputations are mostly formed by one's habits and/or characteristics. What you continually do forms a reputation of what others think of you. Sometimes what people say about you forms your reputation, based on what others perceive of you, whether right or wrong or good or bad. It has been said that a good reputation is hard to create, but it's easy to tear it down.

The Fabulous Wife's reputation goes before her and represents her well because of hardworking hands and her being industrious. Because of all of the things she has done, she is called favored and blessed. Her good reputation even makes her family look good, and people in all places hold her in high esteem. Her husband is honored to call her his wife because of her being virtuous, faithful, hardworking, wise, and a woman of good reputation and character. My children and I see Trish as a blessing to our home and hold her in high esteem. She is "The Fabulous Wife". The way my wife carries herself, treats people, and is profitable in her business allows her to meet the standards of being The Fabulous Wife that Proverbs 31 describes.

As I said, this is neither an exhaustive list nor a be-all end-all for the make-up of The Fabulous Wife. It is the opinion of a godly husband that has seen from experience that these are some of the most important qualities to have in a wife. To all of the men out there, I hope you have found her, and if not, these are some great traits to look for in "The Fabulous Wife".

References

References

All Bible scriptures retrieved from http://www.biblegateway.com

Introduction
Definitions retrieved from http://www.dictionary.com

Chapter 2

What is a Healthy Marriage? Retrieved from http://yourdivorcequestions.org

Connors, Christopher D. (2017, May 26). The 5 Keys to Commitment in a Relationship. Retrieved from https://medium.com/the-mission/the-5-keys-to-commitment-in-relationships-bf20b67abdb4

Becker, Joshua. (2019, October 29). 8 Keys for a Successful and Healthy Marriage. Retrieved from https://www.becomingminimalist.com/8-essentials-for-a-successful-marriage/

Quotes retrieved from http://www.quotefancy.com

Chapter 5

Keeping Score in a Marriage by B. Watson

Chapter 6

Morefield, Scott. (2015, April, 3). Five Reasons Why My Wife Should Obey Me. Retrieved from http://amorefieldlife.com/2015/04/03/why-should-my-wife-obey-me/

Omartian, Stormie. (2014) The Power of a Praying® Husband. Eugene, OR: Harvest House Publishers.

Everyday Ways to Submit to Your Husband by Sabra Penley

Definitions retrieved from https://www.Dictionary.com

Chapter 7

Love Your Wife According to the Bible. (2019, September 27). Retrieved from https://www.wikihow.com/Love-Your-Wife-According-to-the-Bible

Chapman, Dr. Gary. (2016. February 12). How to Truly Love Your Spouse. Retrieved from https://www.focusonthefamily.com/marriage/how-to-truly-love-your-spouse/

Chapter 8

Pease, Joshua, ???? Retrieved from http://www.thrivingmarriages.org

Chapter 9

Smith, Sylvia. (2018, September 20). *Why Good Sex Matters with Married Couples.* Retrieved from https://www.marriage.com/advice/physical-intimacy/why-good-sex-matters-for-married-couples/

WAYS TO GET OUT OF A 'SEX RUT'. Retrieved from https://www.marriage.com

Why Foreplay Matters Especially for Women. Retrieved from: https://www.webmd.com/sex-relationships/features/sex-why-foreplay-matters-especially-for-women

Donaldson-Evans, Catherine. (2015, May 4). *7 Things About Foreplay Sexperts Really Want You to Know.* Retrieved from https://www.sheknows.com/health-and-wellness/articles/1080124/foreplay-tips-from-sex-experts-for-women/

Chapter 10

Fisher, Mary. (2019, December 19). *3 Reasons Why a Lack of Communication in Marriage Can Be Detrimental.* Retrieved from https://www.marriage.com/advice/communication/3-reasons-why-a-lack-of-communication-in-marriage-can-be-detrimental/

Hlavka, Theda. *10 Rules for Good Communication with Your Husband.* Retrieved from https://www.familylife.com/articles/topics/marriage/staying-married/wives/10-rules-for-good-communication-with-your-husband/

Chapter 11

Stritof, Sheri. (2019, October 29). *How to Practice Forgiveness in Marriage.* Retrieved from https://www.verywellmind.com/forgiveness-and-letting-go-in-marriage-2300611

Gormley, Charles & Geline. (2018, June 6). *Five Reasons Why You Should Forgive Your Spouse.* Retrieved from http://lifewithgormleys.com/index.php/2018/06/06/forgive-your-spouse/

Chapter 12

Definitions retrieved from https://www.Dictionary.com

Faith, Srong. (2019, February 17). *The Proverbs 31 Woman Explained: 5 Answers You've Been Waiting For.* Retrieved from https://www.gracefulabandon.com/proverbs-31-woman-explained/

Conrad, Nora. (2014, August 7). *Becoming a Proverbs 31 Woman.* Retrieved from https://www.noraconrad.com/blog/becoming-a-proverbs-31-woman

(2019, August 31). *How to Be a Proverbs 31 Wife.* Retrieved from https://www.wikihow.com/Be-a-Proverbs-31-Wife

TRISH MORRISSETTE

THE AUTHOR

FAITH IN A
BARREN LAND

CHRONICLES OF A
Fabulous
LADY

I AM
FAB-ulous
THE JOURNAL

BOOKS BY TRISH M.

If you have never read any of Trish M.'s books, then you are missing out! Outside of her latest release, The Fabulous Wife, check out all the other goodies Trish M. has to offer. If you are ready to be empowered, enlightened, challenged and repositioned for greatness, then you need to grab these goodies! They'll bless your soul!

1. FAITH IN A BARREN LAND

2. CHRONICLES OF A FABULOUS LADY

3. I AM FABULOUS- THE JOURNAL

TRISH MORRISSETTE

COACHING PROGRAMS

FOLLOW ON SOCIAL MEDIA

ACADEMY OF
PROPHETIC PEOPLE

Are you ready to unleash the power of your unique prophetic gift? Are you interested in exploring the possibilities of God's higher dimension? Do you feel like you were meant for something more, but just can't quite understand what that calling is yet? Now is your time! Hear God's voice with more clarity, confidence, and consistency than ever before! We offer two different payment options. $39 a month, or $400 for a year. TEACHINGS, TEACHINGS, AND MORE TEACHINGS! What you will get:• Access to hundreds of lessons provided by Prophetess Trish & the many Ambassadors assigned to the Academy• FB LIVE biweekly LIVE teachings• Workbooks to go with Teachings• APP Private Mastermind Group Facebook• Private Group Prayer & Fasting Sessions Monthly• Bonus Teachings for Kingdom Entrepreneurship• FREE Registration to our "Speak Lord Prophetic MEGA Conferences"• VIP Session when you register for "Elijah Encounter Prophetic Retreats"

TRISH MORRISSETTE

COACHING PROGRAMS

FOLLOW ON SOCIAL MEDIA

@Prophetess Trish Morrissette   @TrishM   @LadyTrishM   @LadyTrishM

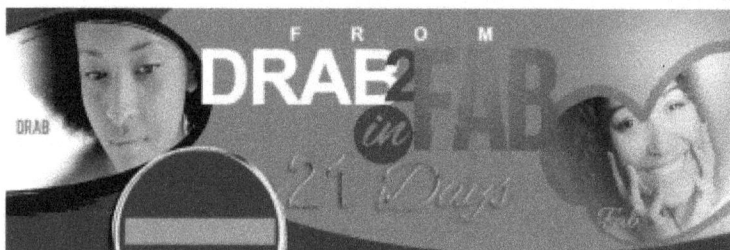

21 Days– Become a Better Person & Change Your Life NOW!

Step-By-Step Daily Life Coaching To Build a Better Life & Be a Better Person in 21 Days!

If you're seeking coaching that will help you CHANGE YOUR THINKING, WHICH IN TURNS CHANGES YOUR LIFE, AND AS A RESULT WILL CHANGE YOUR DESTINY — then this program is for YOU! Eliminate bad habits, get unstuck from ruts, achieve your dreams, get to the next level of success and be who you're destined to be — while living a fulfilling & FABULOUS life!

In 21 days, this virtual training program will give you step-by-step techniques and detailed plans to get every area of your life in order... and eliminate life's roadblocks and obstacles that show up unexpectedly and discourage you from crossing the FINISH LINE into the life, success and happiness you know you deserve.

You'll get:

'21 Day Audio Program–A virtual 21 day personal success system that gives you hard-hitting, well-planned, high-level training to take you from drab to FAB, from chaos to organization, from organization to breakthrough, from breakthrough to maximum success, from maximum success to worldwide leadership!

'21 Day Fab Journal

'21 Day FAB Calendar-Clarity and Direction..... This calendar will give you the guideline that you need to going from living a drab life to living the ultimate FAB life that God has ordained for you to live.

TRISH MORRISSETTE

COACHING PROGRAMS

FOLLOW ON SOCIAL MEDIA

TRISH M MINISTRIES

THE FABULOUS CEO

BUILDING KINGDOM LEADERS & KINGDOM FINANCIERS

Register- www.trishmnow.com

A simply phenomenal, yet powerful coaching program for life, business or ministry all rolled up into a fabulous new training module- "The Fabulous CEO"! It's time to build Kingdom Leaders and Kingdom Financiers like never before! Proverbs 13:22.. A good person leaves an inheritance for their children's children, but a sinner's wealth is stored up for the righteous. Are you ready to work on that inheritance? Whether you're looking to expand your thinking, build your ministry, business, or life, then "The Fabulous CEO" is for you! In this 12 module program, Trish M. challenges the mind first, and then she goes into specific strategies on how to take your life, ministry or business to an ultimate new level! She's adamant about building kingdom leaders and kingdom financiers! If you are ready to learn how to go to the next level of being the CEO of your life, ministry or business, then this program is definitely for you! Trish M has taken her classes from her Association of Fabulous Women program, and put them in this 12 week module to empower the kingdom leaders and kingdom financiers on how they can get to the next level of being all that God called them to be! Topics include AFW Module 1- Understanding & Overcoming Part 1 AFW Module 2- Understanding & Overcoming Part 2 AFW Module 3- The Ultimate Success Part 1 AFW Module 4- The Ultimate Success Part 2 AFW Module 5- Building a New Lifestyle Part 1 AFW Module 6- Building a New Lifestyle Part 2 "Branding" AFW Module 7- Building a New Lifestyle Part 3 "The Balancing Act" AFW Module 8- Building a New Lifestyle Part 4 "Keys to Gaining Wealth" AFW Module 9- Building a New Lifestyle Part 5 "The Art of Selling" AFW Module 10- Building a New Lifestyle Part 6 "Webinars 101" AFW Module 11- Building a New Lifestyle Part 7 "Creating the Perfect Lead Magnet" AFW Module 12- Building a New Lifestyle Part 8 "Promoting the Perfect Lead Magnet"

12 weeks of powerful, impactful and enlightening classes that are definitely going to take your life, ministry and business to a fabulous new level!